Past-into-Present Series

CHILDREN

David Kennedy

B. T. BATSFORD LTD   London

First published 1971
© David Kennedy 1971

Filmset by Keyspools Ltd, Golborne, Lancs.

Printed in Great Britain by Billing & Sons Ltd, Guildford, Surrey
for the Publishers
B. T. Batsford Ltd, 4 Fitzhardinge Street, London W1

7134 1769 2

,hi·   ɔe returned on or
          ·te stamped bel⌐

OR 16.9.93

Contents

Acknowledgment   4

List of Illustrations   5

Introduction   7

1   Medieval Child—Miniature Adult   9

2   Princes, 'Prentices and Paupers 1500–1700   18

3   Little Georgian Gentlefolk   28

4   Children of Poverty: Neglect and Welfare
      1700–1900   37

5   Child Workers 1700–1900   48

6   Fortunate Victorians   59

7   The Century of the Child   67

8   The Teen Age   77

Date-Line of Child Life   91

Index   95

Acknowledgment

The author and publishers wish to thank the following for the illustrations appearing in this book:
The Trustees of the British Museum for fig. 3; The Bodley Head Ltd. for fig. 43; The Courtauld Institute of Art for fig. 2; Fox Photos Ltd. for fig. 52; Mansell Collection for figs. 14, 16, 18–20, 23–4, 28–32, 35, 36, 37b, 38, 39b, 45, 46; Methuen and Co. Ltd. for fig. 4; Popperfoto for figs. 57–9; Radio Times Hulton Picture Library for figs. 6, 7, 10, 11, 13, 15, 17, 25–7, 33, 34, 37a, 39a, 40–2, 44, 47, 49–51, 53–6; Victoria and Albert Museum for figs. 12 and 21.

List of Illustrations

1 Anglo-Saxon family group   9
2 Nurse with swaddled child   10
3 Fourteenth-century wayfarers   11
4 Children's dress of the
   fourteenth century   12
5 Damoiselles and young bachelors   14
6 Child iron-workers   15
7 Children catching butterflies   16
8 A game of Hoodman blind   17
9 Mother and child in sixteenth
   century   19
10 Horn-book   20
11 Early boys' school   21
12 Girl's sampler, 1839   22
13 Tudor family group   23
14 Puritan family   24
15 Sixteenth-century games   25
16 Children of Charles I   26
17 Polite, well-mannered children,
    1742   28
18 Parents neglecting their duties   30
19 Children's picture book   31
20 Wealthy children at play   32
21 Georgian doll's house   32
22 Aspects of education, by
    Rowlandson   34
23 Meeting between rich and poor
    children   35
24 Thomas Coram   38
25 Village dame school   40
26 'Ragged' school, Portsmouth   41
27 Dining-hall of orphanage, 1869   42
28 Playroom of a London crèche   43
29 Tothill Boys' Prison   44
30 Searching for homeless boys, 1871   45
31 Free dinners in Whitechapel   46
32 Country children   48
33 Boy sweep and master   50
34 Factory children at Sunday
    School   51
35 Girl 'hurrier' in coal mines   53
36 Watch boy   53
37 Children in brickmaking trade   54
38 A tailoring family in 1863   56
39 Street-trading children   57
40 Nurse and baby   59
41 Advertisement for prams, 1897   60
42 Nursery rocking horse   61
43 Girls' hats and clothes, 1889   62
44 Victorian middle-class family   64
45 Doll's house, 1898   65
46 Toy shop and 'penny plains'   65
47 Rich and poor families, 1912   68
48 Victim of violent assault   69
49 Children's street games   71
50 Sailor-suit, Edwardian style   72
51 Investiture of a scout   72
52 Evacuation of school children,
    1939   75
53 Child welfare clinic   77
54 Day nursery at lunchtime   78
55 Teaching a deaf child   79
56 Exercise in a Borstal   81
57 Dance hall in the 'fifties   83
58 Teenage cults   84–5
59 Girls' fashions   86

Introduction

What a contrast there is between the average British child of today and the poor wretch of little more than a hundred years ago. Now he is healthy not diseased, well-fed not undernourished, protected not neglected, educated not exploited. Our society has come to realise that its future depends on the quality of its younger generation. Hence governments in this century have gradually developed a complex network of legislation. There are laws to protect children from mistreatment or abandonment by their parents. The National Health Service provides pre-natal and infant care services. Older children receive school medical and dental care. Education is provided for everyone till at least 15. Any child deprived of a normal home life can be taken into care by the local authority. Even youngsters' recreation is catered for by play-centres, adventure playgrounds and libraries.

Unlike our ancestors we are able to prevent or cure children's diseases because of the recent remarkable advances in scientific and medical knowledge. More-over, invention and industrialisation have made us an affluent nation with enough wealth to ensure that most of our children are properly fed and cared for. Equally important, we now recognise that each child passes through many stages of development, that he is continually changing and adapting to the society in which he is a newcomer. We know that his childhood experiences will largely determine the nature of his adult character and personality.

However, though we know more about the nature of children than ever before, we have less confidence in our ability to rear them successfully than the parents of previous centuries. Medieval parents had no such doubts about their ability or the methods they used. They barely recognised the existence of childhood: once babies were out of the helpless stage they were dressed and treated as grown-ups and were expected to begin adult work. Methods of upbringing were simple, with constant beatings and stories about hell to frighten youngsters into adult Christian behaviour.

Though they may seem heartless to us, most parents did love their children: they felt they had to insist on harsh punishment, the strictest obedience and polite-ness for the youngster's own good. Parents did not openly show affection because it was believed that this would make the child soft. Youngsters were discouraged from toys and games. However, it is in a child's nature to play and they usually did so whenever they could. It is delightful to notice that some of their games still excite children today.

From Tudor times wealthy parents slowly began to perceive that instead of pushing little ones into adult society they should allow them a longer childhood with a school education, the pleasure of a few toys and openly expressed parental love.

However, these were the lucky youngsters. The great majority of ordinary children were expected to work and earn almost as soon as they could walk. Society did not grant that every youngster had the right to a childhood, an education and state protection from starvation, mistreatment and over-work. Certainly the country was not wealthy enough to feed and clothe all of them. Ignorance about medicine, disease and methods of infant rearing were a further hindrance to effective child-care. Tudor governments did attempt a national solution to the problem of vagrant and destitute children, but the size of the problem overwhelmed them and during the two succeeding centuries the burden was left to a few humane individuals.

The wastage of child life was enormous as eighteenth- and early nineteenth-century society and government refused to accept responsibility for saving the nation's children. For this reason much of the history of children is one of pain, suffering and neglect. Not until Victorian times do we see society beginning to realise how disastrous the wastage of life was to the economy. Only then do we see the dawn of a national conscience, of state responsibility for the protection of the most helpless, yet potentially the most valuable members of the society.

1 Medieval Child—Miniature Adult

Children have always been the most vulnerable members of a community. They are the first to suffer when there is starvation, disease or war, for they are physically weak, inexperienced and dependent on adult aid and protection. For youngsters of prehistoric times life was exceptionally precarious and the chances of survival very small. Old Stone Age man lived primarily by hunting. As soon as his children could walk they had to become useful to their parents and learn the techniques of hunting. Otherwise, they would have to be abandoned or killed because adults themselves were struggling for survival and could not bear the burden of a helpless child for long.

By Neolithic times, life was easier. Man had become mainly a cultivator and hence his child's labour was more valuable. Nevertheless, children were still murdered by their parents, sometimes for superstitious reasons. The day of birth was very important and magic and potions were used to guarantee birth on a particular day. Anglo-Saxons thought the first day of the moon most fortunate: 'A child born on that day is sure to live and prosper.' Friday was an unlucky day and often it was felt better to kill Friday's child than to allow him to grow up to a life of misfortune. The early Anglo-Saxons also carried out tests to discover whether an infant had the necessary courage to face the hardships of life. He was placed on a sloping roof or the bough of a tree. If he laughed he was taken down and reared, whereas signs of fear and crying meant death.

The treatment of infants

1 An Anglo-Saxon family group; the elder of the boys has reached the age at which he is allowed to have at least a mimic sword.

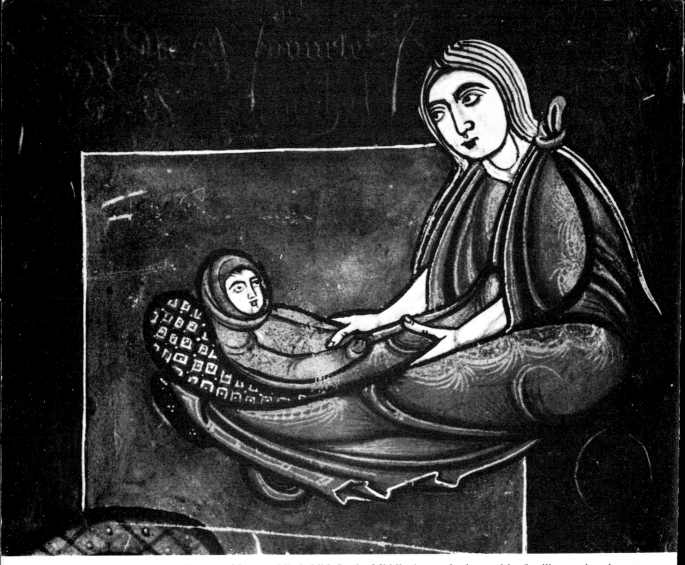

2 A nurse with a swaddled child. In the Middle Ages only the wealthy families employed nurses for their children; the swaddling, however, often did more harm than good – the baby here looks as if he could hardly move an inch.

Wealthy parents employed nurses for their infants. The first task was to swaddle the new-born baby. Its limbs were washed and rubbed with salt and honey and it was wrapped tightly in bands of cloth leaving only the head free to move. This custom was to avert the common complaint of rickets, to ensure the limbs grew straight. In fact, it meant that for two years the infant's limbs remained weak from lack of use. Another example of misguided treatment was the remedy sometimes applied to children who were backward with talking: 'For him that may not speak well give him to drink hounds tongue.'

Until seven years of age, the child led a protected, carefree existence with his nurse and mother in her chambers. They taught him the ABC, Paternoster and enough Latin to follow the church services, and he would soon pick up rhymes, such as *Humpty Dumpty* which is of Saxon origin. Peasant youngsters did not get such attention. They were not swaddled, had no cradle but were lain to sleep on the floor by the fire. Evidence from Anglo-Saxon manuscript pictures suggests that children were left to crawl around the house and among the cattle and went naked until they could walk.

The infant death-rate was tragically high. Plague and fevers were endemic in medieval times. Surgery and medicine were extremely primitive and in any case disease was considered a punishment for sin. Parents believed that many children were created so that a few could be preserved. We have no figures for medieval infant mortality but there are clues. Five children of Henry III died in infancy, four of Edward III and seven of Edward I. If so many royal children perished, what chance for the peasant child?

Many youngsters died through neglect. For example, in the seventh century an ecclesiastical law states: 'If a woman place her infant by the hearth and a man put water in the cauldron and it boil over and the child be scalded to death, the woman must do penance for her negligence.' The need for a special code of laws suggests that this must have been a frequent occurrence.

Numerous accidents to children are recorded in medieval coroners' rolls. For instance, a Canterbury coroner fined the parents of three children who were drowned; one infant was burnt in its cradle; another was accidentally shot by an archer at practice; and many cases tell of infants eaten by swine. Perhaps cruellest of all, we read of beggars who deliberately broke their children's bones and caused deformities in order to win pity and scrounge alms.

The majority of parents were not deliberately cruel but, on the other hand, none of them showed the sentimental care and affection for children which we find in most families in present-day society. Today, a family's main concern is for the well-being and success of the children, whereas in the wealthy medieval family individuals were not important. Instead the chief interests were the family honour and the advancement of family fortune. Children were merely the spokes of a wheel. Parents did want success for their offspring but for the sake of the family not the children.

The nature of family life

3 Fourteenth-century wayfarers and their children.

There were two additional reasons why parents did not show sentimental affection. They did not wish to become attached to children who were most likely to die very young anyway. Secondly, marriages were made for the sake of family fortune not for love, and so parents were unlikely to be very loving towards their children. Mothers frequently left the job of breast-feeding to a wet-nurse. In manuscript illustrations of breast-feeding the child is held vertically—no sign of cuddling.

Tenderness would have a bad effect on the child: one medieval writer insisted that 'fondness and familiarity breed contempt and irreverency in children'. Instead parents should demand humble obedience. Father in particular was regarded with a mixture of awe and reverence. There was no familiarity. Children spoke to their parents in very respectful tones. Let us listen to William Stonor addressing his father: 'My right reverent and worshipful father, I recommend me

4 Different kinds of dress worn by children in the fourteenth century.

12

unto your good fatherhood in the most humble ways I can or may, humbly beseeching your good fatherhood of your daily blessing.' Try it on your dad!

Fifteenth-century books on behaviour indicate what was expected of the youngster. The *Babees Book* (1475) advises a boy to bow and say 'Godspeed' to everyone when he enters the great hall. It adds:

> Take no seat but be ready to stand until you are bidden to sit down. Keep your hands and feet at rest. Do not claw your flesh or lean against a post in the presence of your lord. Make obeisance always to your lord when you answer, otherwise stand as still as a stone until he speak to thee.

The principal aim in upbringing was to subdue the child, for all behaviour books insist on the importance of silence and immobility. A typical book on girl's behaviour is *How the Good Wife taught her Daughter*. A girl must not laugh too loud, yawn too wide, walk too fast or jerk her shoulders about. The book emphasises industry and respectability, and even tells the girl how to deal with her own disobedient children when she is married:

> *If thy children be rebel and will not bow them low,*
> *If any of them misdo neither curse nor blow;*
> *But take a smart rod and beat them in a row*
> *Till they cry mercy and their guilt well know.*

No children escaped frequent beatings. Parents believed them to be so stubborn and proud that they had to be beaten into a state of humility and obedience before their education could commence. Even little King Henry VI, a most meek and obedient child, was not spared the rod. The Privy Council directed his governor, the Earl of Warwick, to beat him reasonably from time to time. One mother, Agnes Paston, instructed her son's schoolmaster to 'truly belash him till he will amend'.

This harsh treatment became more severe at seven years of age. Medieval people believed that at this age childhood ceased and youngsters became miniature adults. From now on they had to act as adults—or be beaten till they did. The upper and middle classes believed that these lessons could best be learnt away from home in another household. Middle-class boys went to live with a craftsman as his apprentice, and aristocratic boys and girls became pages or 'chambrières' in a noble's household. A visiting Venetian ambassador was very shocked by this system and he wrote:

> The want of affection in the English is strongly manifested towards their children; for after having kept them at home till they arrive at the age of seven or nine years at the utmost, they put them out, both males and females, to hard service in the houses of other people, binding them generally for another seven or nine years . . . and few are born who are exempted from this fate for everyone, however rich he may be, sends away his children into the houses of others, whilst he, in return, receives strangers into his own.

However, this Italian visitor had misunderstood parents' motives. Aristocratic children were 'boarded out' because their chances of advancement or profitable marriage would be greatly increased in the house of a lord or rich patron. It was the ideal place for a boy to learn the two basic lessons of his training. These were the art of serving others as a means of furthering himself and the good manners of a knight. He started as a page. He learnt how to carve meat and wait on his lord at table, to sing and dance, to train in the arts of war, hunting and falconry. At 15 or 16 he became a squire and later took the vows of knighthood and received his golden spurs.

It was equally important for girls to live in an influential aristocratic household. The choice of household was vital because her hopes of a good marriage depended on meeting wealthy men of important position. These girl boarders were called 'damoiselles' or 'chambrières'. During the earlier part of the day they remained in their chambers carding wool, spinning (this is the source of our term spinster), weaving wool and making articles of dress or decoration. After dinner until supper they joined the young males in the chambers or garden.

Fourteen was the normal marrying age. Parents picked the partners with the sole aim of advancing family fortunes. Important heirs were sometimes betrothed very young. John Rigmardin endured such a ceremony when aged three. He had to repeat the words of the priest and in the middle he declared he would 'learn no more that day'—but he did finish! Heirs whose parents died became wards—that is, a lord controlled their property while they were minors—and frequently the guardian arranged their marriage for his own profit.

Aristocratic girls without a dowry had little chance of marriage and were usually sent to a convent. Daughters of the wealthy town classes were more fortunate. They had more freedom to choose a marriage partner and if they remained

5 Damoiselles with young bachelors in a noble household. These young girls were 'boarded out' in the hope that they could meet and marry eligible, wealthy young men.

6 Child iron-workers of the fourteenth century – a distinct contrast to the previous illustration.

unmarried could go out to work as a seamstress or embroiderer.

The sons of the wealthy townsmen worked in their father's trade or were apprenticed around seven years of age. Apprenticeship developed during the thirteenth century as a system of industrial training. In the contract of service—the indenture—the master promised to feed and clothe the boy, give him a place in his own house and teach him every branch of the craft. In return, the boy's father paid money and goods each year and his son worked for seven years with his master. The system was later adopted by the trade gilds and in time made compulsory by them as a method of regulating entry into a craft. Some gilds supervised their apprentices very closely. Ironmongers made a by-law as to the dress and appearance of apprentices whose hair had not to grow too long. That sounds familiar! Many apprentices were not even free to do as they pleased after work. At Carlisle they could not go out after 10 o'clock except on their master's business.

Peasant children

No country boy could become an apprentice to a craft unless his father was wealthy and owned land of 40s annual value. This did not mean he did no work as a child—just the opposite. Soon after he had learnt to walk he would be given simple tasks like scaring birds and running errands. Later he worked as a ploughboy or shepherd, fed the hens and pigs, and learnt pruning, hedging and ditching. Until the late Middle Ages most peasants were unfree men, holding land on condition of personal service. The labour of their children was often definitely contracted for in these agreements between overlord and villein. So children had to

15

remain as farm labourers and could not leave the district.

Girls also began work in the fields at an early age. In addition, they helped their mothers to look after the younger children and assisted with the incessant tasks of cooking, spinning and weaving wool, washing, plaiting straw and reeds and collecting and peeling rushes for lighting. Occasionally girls were apprenticed to embroiderers, glove-makers and other craftsmen. Children of poor labourers sometimes became servants in the houses of their more fortunate neighbours. A bondswoman was made to do all the hardest work 'toylynge and slubberynge' and was 'kepte lowe under the Yoeke of thraldom and servage'.

Play

Though working hours were long children did have plenty of holy days for play. Their few toys were simple in nature: whips and tops, balls, skipping ropes, hobby-horses, toy windmills. Wealthy boys had toy soldiers or miniature weapons and armour. The majority without toys played games copied from their parents. They played at Kayles, in which a stick was thrown at skittles, or at Quoits, Trap Ball, Prisoner's Base, Hoodman Blind (Blindman's Buff) or Hot Cockles. In the last-named game one person knelt blindfold and was hit by the other players in turn until he guessed the name of the striker who then had to take his place. Even rougher were the mass games of football.

Too soon the holy day ended and children returned to the fields. Peasant children's only legitimate escape from a lifetime of bondage was to become a priest. A boy would start as a server to the village priest, who in return might teach him the elements of Latin so that he could follow the services and join in the responses. Eventually, the boy would apply to the manor court for permission to enter the priesthood as a novice.

School

Until the fourteenth century the priests were traditionally responsible for the education of all youngsters. Rectors at every large monastery, hospital, cathedral

7 Fourteenth-century children at play, using their hoods to catch butterflies. The butterflies are not drawn to scale!

8 A game of Hoodman Blind. A player was blindfolded by reversing his hood, and his friends then knotted their own hoods to hit him. The blindfolded player then had to guess who the striker was, and if he guessed correctly, they changed places.

and college had for long been responsible for the education of choristers and novices. The children of the nobility occasionally received tuition in the monasteries. More often, boys of this class were taught by masters in the great households to which their parents had sent them. We have seen already that training in good manners and in knightly exercises were of first importance, but the pages also learnt Latin, perhaps other languages, and certainly learnt to dance, sing and to play musical instruments. Such was the demand for education from the gentry and rising yeoman classes by the end of the fourteenth century that new schools opened all over the country. For example, 24 grammar schools were founded between 1363 and 1400. Previously, education had been mainly the church's responsibility. Now laymen began to play their part in founding schools and teaching. There were gild schools, municipal schools and schools opened in hospitals through the bequests of wealthy men.

This development is very significant. Parents were beginning to reject the theory that children learnt best by service as a page or apprentice. A minority dimly recognised for the first time in England that youngsters required special treatment and prolonged childhood instead of the dubious honour of miniature adulthood at seven years of age.

Further Reading
John Bagley, *Life in Medieval England*
Alfred Duggan, *Growing up with the Norman Conquest*
P. M. Kendall, *The Yorkist Age. Daily life during the Wars of the Roses*

2 Princes, 'Prentices and Paupers
1500–1700

Birth customs A baby's birth was invariably a signal for elaborate celebration and ritual in all but the poorest Tudor and Stuart families. Friends drank wine and made music with the father, toasted the health of the baby when its first cries were heard, made money gifts and sometimes lit a bonfire. Among the less wealthy a 'groaning-cake' was cut up and distributed for luck.

Superstitions about birth abounded. The baby had to be wrapped in an old piece of cloth at first, for anything new would bring bad luck. Anxious relatives took careful note of the position of the stars as the time of birth approached. When labour began the church bells were rung to frighten away evil spirits for the new-born baby might be 'overlooked', that is bewitched by the glance of an evil eye. Also, fairies were fond of beautiful children and might attempt to steal the child. The safest protection against these dangers was christening and so this ceremony was usually performed within a few days of birth. The parents were careful to pick a name of 'good significance' for the child. Biblical names were popular, very religious parents favouring Faith, Hope or Temperance, whereas extreme Puritans in the seventeenth century inflicted incredible names like 'Sorry-for-sin' or 'If-Christ-had-not-died-thou-hadst-been-damned'.

Sad to say the majority of parents were soon attending their child's funeral. A town child had a one in three chance of reaching the age of one, and thereafter the same one in three chance of reaching five. The survival rate to the age of five was 11 children out of 100 live births from all classes. Smallpox, plague, typhus, typhoid, measles and the new 'sweating sickness' or influenza ravaged the child population. Many more died from deficient feeding or an unpalatable diet. Too soon mothers put their babies on diets low in nutritional value. A diet of fine flour or bread mixed with milk was given in a pewter pap-boat. When fully weaned the baby had bread crusts, milk and soups and the occasional meat-bone to help with teething.

Many poverty-stricken parents could not afford even these foods and the mothers were too undernourished to be able to suckle their babies and had thus to abandon them. Parish records have numerous entries recording the burial of deserted children found dead on the roads from exposure and starvation. During the Tudor period, London began schemes to rescue these destitute children and many towns followed London's lead. Christ's Hospital opened in 1552 with accommodation for 500 abandoned youngsters. So many foundlings were dumped at the gates of Christ's Hospital that restrictions soon had to be placed on entry: henceforth only legitimate children were admitted and, later, only the orphans of freemen and citizens. Bridewell was an institution in London which provided

9 A sixteenth-century mother with her child, from a drawing by Holbein.

technical training for the older child. Relief schemes began in other larger towns, such as Bristol, Norwich, York, Exeter and Plymouth, but they generally failed through lack of finance and because they attracted overwhelming numbers from the poor of the surrounding areas.

In 1597, an Act for the Relief of the Poor finally made the parish or municipality responsible for the care of all orphans and destitute children during their early years. Tremendous organisation and funds were needed for such a plan to operate but neither materialised and many areas neglected their duties. Nevertheless the Elizabethans had shown a new concern for protecting child life which contrasted sharply with medieval attitudes that disease and death were God's punishments for sin and could not be avoided.

Meanwhile wealthy parents were showing increasing sympathy and affection for their infants and a novel delight in their quality of childishness. Babies were

Schooling of the wealthy

dandled on their mother's knee to *See-saw Margery Daw* or *Ride a cock-horse*. They had bells, rattles and a rag doll for play, and corals to help them cut their first teeth. Some households had a separate room, a nursery, for the youngsters. Nurses sang lullabies and rocked them to sleep in cradles of solid wood with deep rockers. Infants picked up speech from nursery jingles. A poem of 1574 reveals that the child's first words were invariably the same as those of our infants nowadays:

> *'Dad dad' for father first they give,*
> *and 'bead' they teach for bread:*
> *And when they teach him drink to ask*
> *then 'din' to him is said.*

The reciting of *This little pig went to market* or *One, two, Buckle my Shoe* taught them to count and they were soon singing *Old King Cole* or *Sing a Song of Sixpence* or listening to the story of *The Babes in the Wood*.

However, this period of spoiling did not last long. Education began early. Almost as soon as they could speak they were taught to read by their mother or nurse, who used a horn-book. Girls' needlework lessons on hemming and stitching started when they could hold a needle. Lucy Hutchinson tells us: 'I was taught to speak French and English together. . . . By the time I was four years old I read English perfectly.'

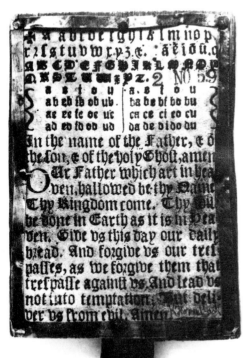

10 A seventeenth-century horn book, with the ABC and the Lord's Prayer, which the youngster had to learn by heart.

11 The scene in a boy's school in the sixteenth century. The master on the left is punishing one of the pupils, while behind, another of the boys reads aloud to the rest of the class. On the right the boys are also reading and no doubt keeping a watchful eye on the switch in the master's hand!

Admittedly she was exceptional but advanced education did begin for most children at four. A boy experienced the ceremony of 'breeching' at this age. He shed his baby petticoats, left the nursery altogether and stepped out dressed as a little gentleman. However, as we mentioned in the last chapter, many parents were beginning to reject the notion of forcing the child into early adulthood. Instead parents appreciated the necessity for long schooling. They realised children could not learn all that was needed for adult life just by being with adults. The period of childhood had to be extended and youngsters trained in schools for future success in society. The middle classes were the first to perceive that the best schooling for commercial and political success was practical education in languages, reading and logic, and a moral and intellectual training in classics. Equally, the Renaissance excited a love of learning to replace the previous aristocratic scorn of 'clerkly accomplishments'. Many now ridiculed chivalry and called it 'open manslaughter and bold bawdry'. The knight and his fighting skill were giving place to the gentleman and his intellectual skills.

There were private, courtly schools and tutors for the nobility; endowed public and gild schools with a wider curriculum for both the nobility and middle classes; and finally there were grammar schools. Many of the last-mentioned were founded in the sixteenth century by generous merchants for the companies, particularly after 1547 when Henry VIII's dissolution of the monasteries had forced the closure of so many schools. Many were labelled free schools but in practice they generally catered for middle-class boys who attended from around seven years of age. The training was mainly classical. The master taught the boys to speak and write Latin, and later introduced Greek, Hebrew and a study of good literature.

Elizabeth's reign marks the beginning of the change from the 'boarding-out' system to attendance at public schools for boys of the nobility. The change was gradual and some parents preferred to appoint a private tutor or send their children to courtly schools where music, singing, dancing, fencing and training in manners and courtesy were still stressed.

Most aristocratic girls were educated at home by tutors, the family chaplain or governesses. They continued their needlework. At seven or eight years of age they practised a variety of stitches on linen samplers and made an elaborate dressing-box before they were 13. In later centuries girls were merely trained in social graces to attract husbands who expected their wives to be more ignorant and irresponsible than themselves. Not so the gentlemen of Tudor and Stuart times.

12 From the Tudor and Stuart times it was the custom for girls to practise their needlework on linen samplers, and they generally stitched into them some kind of Christian message or verse. This sampler was made in 1839.

13 A wealthy Tudor family. The fact that the children are in the centre of the group indicates the new importance attached to proper family life from the sixteenth century onwards.

They sought wives skilled in reading and writing and a foreign language, who were able to supervise their husband's estate. Wives would have to manage the servants, make drugs and understand surgery, provide all the household's cloth and clothes and supervise all the cooking and brewing. ✗

Medieval youngsters had left home at seven, parents rarely saw them again and the responsibility for rearing the child passed to others. By the early seventeenth century aristocratic and middle-class children were educated at home or returned each school holiday, so parents had to take responsibility for the children's welfare. At the same time, churchmen were preaching that children were fragile creatures of God who had to be safeguarded and deterred from evil. This task too fell to parents.

Parents: loving but strict

Most parents were quite happy to take on these new burdens and the nature of family life changed as attention began to focus on the children. Evidence can be found in the paintings of the time. Proud parents commissioned numerous child

23

portraits and by the seventeenth century for the first time there are many paintings of family groups with everyone grouped *round* the child, or with mother and father holding a child. Also, there are many descriptions of the celebrations when schoolboys returned for the holidays. Parents now worried about the education, career and future prospects of their offspring.

Though many parents were tender and affectionate, children were still brought up very strictly. Obedience, respect and courtesy were essential for the child: they addressed parents as 'Sir' and 'Madam' and stood up when their parents entered the room. Religious ideas had an important influence on upbringing. Nowadays we regard children as basically innocent: to the Tudors they brimmed with original sin and could only be plucked from the threat of hell by severe training. What we would regard as little faults were labelled grave sins and merited a beating or hours in a dark cupboard.

Puritan ministers published a series of little books warning children not to rely on God's mercy or their own salvation: one said, 'Children are not too little, they are not too little to go to hell'; and another, 'Children who lye, play the truant and

14 A Puritan father instructs his children in religion. For all the increasing affection towards children, the sons and daughters of Puritans were brought up in a very strict way, taught to memorize large parts of the Bible and the Prayer Book and to respect parental authority.

15 Youngsters at play in the sixteenth century. It is easy to recognise a rattle and hobby horse. On the right a boy is blowing bubbles through a reed, while his friends are trying to catch the bubbles on cushions.

break the Sabbath will go into everlasting burning'. These threats must have turned some youngsters into terrified creatures. Puritans believed that the devil had to be whipped out of children. Fortunately most parents did not fully accept Puritan advice and whipping became less severe in Stuart times. Most parents, however, continued to equip youngsters to meet the challenges of the devil by making them learn by heart the catechism, and sections from the Scriptures and prayer-book.

Puritan parents discouraged play and games but most other parents allowed their youngsters to run wild after lessons in games like 'Here we go round the Mulberry Bush', 'Oranges and Lemons', hide and seek, hunt the ring, hopscotch, leapfrog, see-saw and marbles. The most popular chasing game was Barley Break, also called the Last Couple in Hell. Three equal strips were marked out with a couple in each strip. The couple in the middle were in hell and were the chasers. If you were caught you exchanged places with them.

These games were played by children from all classes of society because little or no equipment was necessary. However, in most other respects the life of the rich and poor children contrasted very sharply. Youngsters of the poorest classes were expected to work from four or five years of age and most other boys became apprentices.

25

Apprenticeship   In 1563 the Elizabethan Statute of Artificers had made a seven-year apprenticeship compulsory for all who wanted to be trained in an industrial craft. In the towns merchants and tradesmen could only apprentice boys whose fathers possessed 40s freehold or 60s in the case of high-class trades, such as goldsmiths. The apprentices worked the same hours as their masters, though there were many holidays for saints' days. Usual summer working hours were from 5 in the morning till 7 or 8 at night and in winter from dawn till dusk. Masters had strict control over the apprentices' activities. In his indentures the boy promised to be of good conduct and civility, to abstain from dice and card games and the 'haunting' of taverns. Sports and games, music and dancing were often forbidden to apprentices. In 1697 a Newcastle company forbade apprentices 'to get to fencing or dancing school, nor to music houses, lotteries, or playhouses, neither to keep any sort of horses, dogs for hunting, or fighting cocks'. No doubt this is a list of the favourite pastimes of the lads, who would secretly evade the orders. They particularly objected to instructions not to wear lace, velvet and embroidery, or 'their hair long nor locks at their eares like ruffians'.

The children of poorer men had to enter the inferior trades and train to be a carpenter, mason or ploughwright. Outside the gilds were many low-skilled and unskilled labourers such as carters, porters and woodmongers who needed children as cheap assistants. These youngsters formed a large proportion of all juvenile workers and could rely on no gild authorities to supervise their welfare. Yet even they were luckier than the pauper apprentices.

Pity the pauper   The policy of dealing with the children of paupers by apprenticeship began in Henry VIII's reign. There had been a general increase in vagrancy, begging and crime in the early sixteenth century, repressive policies failed and for the first time the State began to take an interest in the welfare of vagrant children in the hope of reforming them, so saving trouble in the future. An Act of 1536 instructed authori-

16   The children of Charles I in a painting by Van Dyck. On the left is Charles, Prince of Wales, next to James, Duke of York, and Princess Mary. The baby, James, has not yet reached the age of 'breeching', but the other two are dressed, as the custom then demanded, as miniature adults.

ties in every parish to take healthy begging children between the ages of 5 and 14 and apprentice them into husbandry or other crafts, so that they could work and not beg when adults. However, the main aim was not to teach the child a trade but to remove him from a degrading way of life. Children between 12 and 16 who refused service or later returned to begging were to be openly whipped.

The Act certainly did not reduce the problem of vagrancy for in the following years it grew to disturbing proportions, and the authorities desperately passed another act in 1547. Under this Act anyone could take a vagrant child from its parents on the sole condition that he swore before a justice, a constable and two neighbours to bring up the child in honest work. Any runaway child who was caught could be put in chains and made a slave. Within two years the severity of this Act was reduced and safeguards against ill-treatment of the children were introduced.

In the Act for the Relief of the Poor, 1597, churchwardens and overseers of the poor were to apprentice not just vagrant and destitute children but all whose parents did not seem able to maintain them. Frequently the youngsters were bound out to men who could barely support them, had no care for their duties, and who were in the poorer trades, such as cobbling and pin-making, in which competition was fierce and the conditions of work miserable.

It was no one's business to see that pauper apprentices were not overworked and underfed. Few masters felt it their duty to train a boy in a trade, but just to keep him alive. By the end of the seventeenth century the practice of 'dumping' had become popular. The parish officers paid sums of money to masters in another parish to take their pauper youngsters as apprentices. Thus, the children became the responsibility of another parish; they were miles from home and the master, who had accepted them only for the money reward, often deliberately ill-treated them till they ran away.

What a contrast this is to the affection and care wealthy youngsters enjoyed. Even sadder is the fact that, though the Elizabethans had at least attempted to save the pauper child, the Stuarts had become discouraged by the overwhelming size and cost of the task and most Georgians of the next century showed even less concern for this daily wastage of life.

Further Reading
Christina Hole, *English Home Life 1500–1800*
Olive Dunlop, *English Apprenticeship and Child Labour*
Elizabeth Godfrey, *Social Life under the Stuarts*

3 Little Georgian Gentlefolk

Wealthy Georgian parents could buy their children an education, toys, clothes, a pleasant nursery, attentive nurse-maids and, later, a suitable job or husband. What they could not purchase for their youngsters was good health, so important in an age when three-quarters of all English children died before they were six. Certainly medical remedies and advice were for sale, but most were misconceived or even dangerous since understanding of medicine and disease was still rudimentary.

Feeding baby

Infants suffered mistaken treatment from birth. Scottish nurses gave new-born babies a spoonful of gin as their first drink and then dipped them in cold water whatever the time of year. Many believed babies were born hungry and so the poor infant was straightaway stuffed with bread and water or a posset of flour and sugar.

Many mothers refused to breast-feed their children and the popular alternative was 'pap'—a mixture of bread and milk or rice flour and arrowroot mixed with milk. Cows' milk was distrusted as too heavy a food and asses' milk was preferred. If the baby cried it was immediately fed. The pap was given in a 'bubbly-pot' made of earthenware or horn with a sponge inside which regulated the flow but unfortunately also harboured germs.

A pioneer in child welfare, Dr Cadogan, published *An Essay on Nursing* in

17 Polite, well-mannered children in 1742, the offspring of Daniel Graham, Apothecary to Chelsea Hospital.

1747, in which he insisted on the importance of breast-feeding and the danger of heavy paps. Sir William Fordyce wrote in 1773:

> They are fed on meat before they have got their teeth, and what is, if possible, still worse, on biscuits not fermented, or buttered rolls, or tough muffins floated in oiled butter, or calves-feet jellies, or strong broths, yet more calculated to load all their powers of digestion.

Dr Hans Sloane was convinced of the mortal dangers of feeding by hand and demanded breast-feeding even for foundlings. He emphasised that one-third of all who died each year were children under two and that the outstanding cause was unsuitable food. In a three-month survey of foundlings he found that only five breast-fed children out of 26 died, whereas 34 out of 63 fed on pap died. Fortunately, by the end of the eighteenth century, it became commonly accepted practice for mothers to feed their own infants, though wet-nurses were still employed and some wealthy parents sent their pre-school children to be brought up by cottage wives in the country.

Survivors of infancy still faced many hazards—smallpox, typhus, fever and scarlet fever and consumption, though by 1800 vaccination was checking the prevalence of smallpox. Children had to endure appalling so-called cures: for coughs 'two or three snails boiled in barley water or tea water', or a broth made of 'old stewed owl and two puppies' and for smallpox 10–40 toads ground into powder. And how would you have fancied a fried mouse to cure whooping cough? Purging, bleeding and blistering were common practice and the daily dose was Daffy's Elixir—a mixture of senna, jalop, carraway seeds and juniper berries in alcohol, treacle and water. Not surprisingly one contemporary protested against 'a few army surgeons who still fancy that a baby's inside is much like a Scotch grenadier's'.

Infant illness

The disease of rickets was the all-too-common consequence of faulty diets and a lack of fresh air and exercise. Raw fruit and fresh vegetables were considered indigestible and bad for children, so there was much scurvy. Mothers constantly worried about infants getting chills and so they wrapped them in tight swaddling bands, overloaded them with clothes, kept them in over-hot rooms away from sunlight and air and seldom bathed them in case they caught a cold.

Until four years of age infants of both sexes wore frocks, after which they changed to small-scale versions of their parents' clothes. In the hope of developing a slim waist little girls had to endure boned corsets, sometimes even having to sleep in them. They were burdened with heavily-embroidered, ankle-length skirts and heavy petticoats and elaborate headdresses. About 1775 sensible parents began to dress their children in clothes specially designed for youngsters—a fashion previously unknown. Little girls wore light, simple, short, high-waisted 'Empire' frocks without petticoats or corsets and their brothers had little coats, loose-fitting trousers and frilled shirts open at the neck.

Parental attitudes

18 This cartoon shows parents neglecting their duties, and allowing
their children to run riot and to
torment animals.

The introduction of children's fashions is just one indication of parents' growing sympathy for the special needs of childhood. More carefree years in the nursery were allowed and older children were given lengthy training before introduction into adult society. In previous centuries children were thought to be full of original sin. Now some parents saw them as radiant innocents who would eventually be spoiled by civilization. A minority of parents even coddled and pampered their children, while others devoted much time to teaching their offspring. The family circle became smaller and more private. Servants were now summoned by a bell, friends usually visited by appointment instead of calling at any hour. Formality within the gentry family was disappearing; children no longer knelt and asked parental blessing, nor remained standing in their fathers' presence; and 'mamma' and 'papa' replaced the cold 'sir' and 'madam'.

We meet opposite attitudes among the many fervently religious middle-class parents who believed that young children were essentially wicked and could only be saved by continual punishment and coercion. John Wesley's parents fed their children sparingly as this soothed angry passions and they taught them to cry softly and fear the rod when they were one year old! Flogging was common in these families for 'the first thing to be done is to conquer their will and to bring them to obedient temper'. Play was frowned on: 'he that plays when he is a child will play when he is a man'; and toys and games were disallowed on Sunday.

Reading, toys
and games

Instead these youngsters were made to read 'improving' books, specially written for them from the 1780s onwards, in which naughty children got just punishments, parents were continually emphasising the sinfulness of their children and reminding them they could be destined for hell. There was a high incidence of sudden death: disobedient children playing with fire were, for example, burnt to death.

Before mid-century, very few books were written for the amusement of children and for adventure stories children generally read chapbooks intended for the adult poor classes. These paper-covered booklets, sold by wandering pedlars, told fairy-tales and recounted the exploits of such heroes as Jack the Giant Killer

19 A children's picture book gives an awful warning to disobedient children who play with fire.

or Saint George. Youngsters also enjoyed adult books like *Gulliver's Travels* or *Robinson Crusoe*. Then in 1744 John Newbery came to London and began publishing the first books for the enjoyment solely of children. His first *A Little Pretty Pocket Book* was a mixture of entertainment and instruction and he went on to publish a whole series of little books.

Many wealthy parents now encouraged their children to play and for the first time it was profitable for some tradesmen to devote their whole business to catering for children. The cheaper toys were hawked around the streets by vendors who blew on a pipe to attract attention. Their top-selling toys were cardboard windmills and horses' heads fastened to the end of sticks. As early as 1738 Martin's Toy and Cap Shop in London was advertising a wide variety of toys. Ever-popular were dolls, dressed in contemporary clothes, with heads of rag, wood, wax or 'china'. On sale too were exquisite and expensive dolls' houses, Noah's Arks, rocking-horses with the upper part in the shape of a horse and the lower part with deep solid rockers; also balls, boats, whistles, monkeys-on-sticks, kites, drums, tops, hoops and Jack-in-the-boxes. The mechanical toy first appeared in the eighteenth century, though it did not reach peak popularity until Victorian times. Two popular ball-games were tip-cat and trap-ball. In both a stick or ball was knocked into the air and then whacked away with a stick.

20 An eighteenth-century painting by George Morland showing wealthy children at play. The little boy is using miniature bellows to blow his ship across the water.

21 A typically ornate – and costly – Georgian doll's house.

Table games, which involved progression along squares with alternating forfeits and rewards depending on a dice-throw, suddenly became popular in mid-century as did instructional games. Stuart children had played with a pack of grammatical cards but now there were card-games of history, geography, arithmetic, heraldry, military science and biography. Board-games covered similar subjects. In the 'Journey through Europe' the players moved counters through the main towns on a map of Europe. Jigsaw puzzles first appeared in the 1760s and the finished picture was a geographical, historical or scriptural subject.

Though there was a wide variety of toys and games, even wealthy children had to be content with just a few. Also, entertainments for children outside the home were limited and the occasional outings were exciting treats. Of course there was always the hawker calling 'Oh Raree Show!' and charging you a halfpenny to gaze at vividly coloured pictures through a peep-hole in his large box. Rivalling him were street singers, musicians and particularly the Punch and Judy shows. Otherwise the outstanding treats were visits to the traditional annual fair or to the more recently established circus.

But these occasions were highspots in a rather dull existence. A 15-year-old, Maria Holyroyd describes her dreary daily routine:

'Genteel accomplishments' for girls

> I get up at 8. I walk from 9 to 10, we then breakfast; about 11 I play on the harpsicord or I draw. I translate, and at 2 walk out again, 3 I generally read, and 4 we go to dine, after dinner we play at Backgammon; we drink tea at 7 and I work or play on the piano till 10, when we have our little bit of supper and 11 we go to bed.

The education of girls had changed fundamentally in aim and method since Tudor and Stuart times. Gone was the methodical grounding in household management and a variety of academic subjects. They were replaced by 'genteel accomplishments'. It was thought unladylike to be able to do anything well. Accomplishments were fake and shallow. Languages were not taught methodically: a jumble of apt phrases were learnt in parrot-fashion just to impress people in conversation. Girls learnt to play only a few show-pieces on the spinet and to sing ballads with easy accompaniments. They made all sorts of fancy pastry, cakes and sauces but did not learn the basic arts of cookery. Embroidery occupied much time but was equally useless since girls only stitched letters of the alphabet on samplers and made no articles of practical use.

By contrast, dancing and deportment were of paramount importance and here at least the teaching was thorough. One little girl remarked that it seemed as if 'making a graceful curtsey was the chief end of human existence'. Girls learnt the correct method of entering and leaving a room, how to leave a carriage, and even how to handle a cup of tea! Correct bearing was regarded as indispensable to social success. Girls had to hold themselves erect and keep a straight back. They were forced to endure tight-lacing, 'straightening boards' strapped to their backs, iron-collars, feet-stocks and neck-swings.

33

The object of her education was to learn to conduct herself gracefully in polite society, which in turn enabled her to pursue the only career open to her — winning a partner and settling to marriage. Genteel accomplishments would impress a man, whereas he would be frightened away if she appeared knowledgeable and well-educated. If she remained a spinster either her parents would have to support her or she would work as a waiting-gentlewoman in another household.

Boys at school ✳ Most wealthy boys were now educated in schools, though private tutors by no means disappeared and, in some cases, they were sent to supervise the boy at his school. Grammar schools had lost favour with the aristocracy and the dreary classical curriculum was unattractive to the middle classes, who began to favour private schools with commercial and vocational subjects on the syllabus.

Some of the aristocracy disapproved of these new subjects. They began to patronise public schools, most of which were for boarders. These schools grew enormously in stature during the century. Most were understaffed. In 1718 Eton had a headmaster and eight assistants to teach 350 boys; Rugby had only six masters for over 200 boys. Masters were forced to use excessive flogging in their struggle to discipline the large numbers. Boys were uncontrolled during their spare time, when they could get drunk and acquire 'a very pretty knowledge of the town'. ✳

Occasionally there were schoolboy rebellions against flogging. In 1797 Rugby schoolboys smashed all the windows, dragged out the school's furniture and books and set fire to them. In 1793 Winchester pupils occupied the building, threw out

22 Two cartoons by Rowlandson depicting the non-academic side of education. On the left we see some youngsters at play at a private school during a break from their studies; on the right, a scene at university as a young undergraduate tries to hide the results of his riotous living from his tutor!

23 Vivid contrasts in this representation of a meeting between rich and poor children. 'Here, poor Boy without a hat', the little girl is saying, 'Take this ha'penny.'

the masters and planted a red cap of liberty on the school tower. There were monitors to keep order but they misused their authority to bully. Southey mentions a boy who was taken away from Charterhouse because he was nearly killed by bullying. He was held in front of a fire till he was scorched and was shut in a trunk till he almost suffocated. Certainly, 'The Charterhouse at that time was a sort of hell upon earth for lower boys'.

Not all schools were so unpleasant and a boy was not bullied for long. The eighteenth century was a violent age and the majority of English children, those of the working class, endured a much harder life with many beginning work at five years old and most children receiving no education at all. At the end of the eighteenth century only the aristocratic and middle-class children had any real childhood at all.

Further Reading

F. Gordon Roe, *The Georgian Child*
Rosamund Bayne-Powell, *The English Child in the Eighteenth Century*

4 Children of Poverty: Neglect and Welfare 1700–1900

Foundlings

It was common practice for poverty-stricken Georgian parents to abandon unwanted infants in the streets, or to kill them and then dump their bodies on dung-heaps to save funeral expenses. If these facts shock us we should remember that Georgian conditions of life bear little comparison to ours. Many parents had to desert their children because they already had other starving offspring; girls who had illegitimate babies received condemnation, not sympathy and help; most infants of poor parents died soon anyway even when the mother struggled to care for the child; and finally society believed that the parents were responsible for their children and no one else had the right to interfere.

If the abandoned infants survived they were taken to the workhouse where they would almost certainly die. Parents could pay a lump sum to parish officials, then hand over and be rid of the child without resorting to murder. Poor law officials boarded out infants with nurses at 1s or 2s a week. A parliamentary committee reported in 1715:

> A great many poor infants are inhumanely suffered to die by the barbarity of the nurses who are a sort of people void of commiseration or religion, hired by the church wardens to take off a burden from the parish at the easiest rates they can and these know the manner of doing it effectually.

Infants were passed like parcels: the parents handed the responsibility to authorities, who in turn paid a nurse, and everyone conveniently ignored the inevitable death which followed. It is easy to be critical of the poor law authorities but they were overwhelmed by numbers without the funds to help even a minority. Perhaps the whole society was to blame since it was unwilling to provide for foundlings 'lest it should encourage vice by making too easy a provision for illegitimate children'.

The welfare work of Coram and Hanway

A retired sea-captain, Thomas Coram, was so appalled at the wastage of life that he determined to help relieve distress by building a Foundling Hospital. In 1741, it opened in temporary accommodation and such was the immediate pressure for places that he had to introduce a ballot and admit only healthy-looking babies. In 1756 he asked for government help because his resources were insufficient to meet the demand. The government was impressed by his hospital's success: since its opening only just over half the children admitted had died, whereas only three to four per cent of workhouse infants survived. The government made a grant on the condition that no infant should be refused admittance. There followed an avalanche of children cartloaded from workhouses all over the country during the next four years. The death-rate jumped to 70 per cent and the hospital's reputa-

24 Thomas Coram with an abandoned infant. In the background is the Foundling Hospital, which he founded so that abandoned children at least had the chance to live and grow instead of being left to die.

tion sank. In 1760, the grant had to be relinquished and admittance limited.

Jonas Hanway, a governor of the Foundling Hospital, hit on another method of saving infants after analysing the death-rates of youngsters in London workhouses. His parliamentary bill of 1767 proposed that all London parish children under six should be boarded out at a minimum cost of 2s 6d, with a bonus of 10s a year for each successful nurse. These attractive terms were the first-ever encouragement to the nurse to preserve the child. As Hanway said, his act caused 'a great deficiency of burials', though it applied only to London.

Workhouses   Poor law officials did not always welcome a reduction of the death-rate for this merely increased the burden on their over-strained resources. In any case, the feeling of responsibility towards children had seriously declined since Tudor times when reformers had had great hopes of ending poverty by education and training. The failure of these hopes and a breakdown in the efficient supervision of poor law administration by the mid seventeenth century led to new attitudes to pauper upbringing. A reduction of costs became the chief concern. Society wished children to earn their own keep, hence the younger paupers were made to spend long hours on unskilled jobs in workhouses.

Very few workhouses made any profit and officials were glad to be able to apprentice children at any time after the age of six and to pay someone else to take their responsibility. Some were shipped to Virginia as servants and later in the century thousands worked in the cotton mills, or as chimney-sweeps. Others were used as cheap farm labour or unpaid servants to large poor families. It was impossible to ensure that pauper apprentices were not mistreated because so many masters were used, children often worked in the privacy of their master's home, and they were apprenticed many miles from their home parish. However an act of 1816 insisted that no London pauper should be bound out more than 40 miles away, and that no child under nine could be apprenticed.

Vagrants and delinquents

When they had received their fee from the overseers many masters mistreated the children and encouraged them to run away to join the hordes of abandoned vagabond children who roamed town and country and lived like savages. Their rudeness had been described by T. Firmin in a pamphlet of 1678: they swore and fought each other over farthings, hurled dirt and stones into passing carriages or at glass windows and whipped horses which sometimes threw their riders. This hooliganism easily degenerated into crime both because there was no effective police system and because the children had to choose between stealing or starvation. At the end of the eighteenth century there were reckoned to be over 3,000 receivers of stolen goods and numerous thieves' kitchens, similar to Fagin's in *Oliver Twist*. Children learnt the art of stealing—first to pick a handkerchief, then a watch and then to pilfer from, and break into, shops.

Criminal punishments were extremely harsh. Children were imprisoned, hanged or transported for minor offences. A few examples will suffice. The prisons were full of infant pickpockets; one youngster is reputed to have cried for his mother on the scaffold; and in 1813 two boys, 10 and 12 years old, were sentenced to seven years' transportation for stealing some warehouse linen.

The continuing failure of this repressive policy prompted sympathetic men of influence to try their own solutions during the eighteenth century. Sir John Fielding took vagrant boys from the streets and settled them on ships of the fleet, where life was extremely tough but temptations to crime were less. He asked the Marine Society under Jonas Hanway for assistance and between 1756 and 1862 the Society fitted out and sent to sea more than 10,000 boys.

Through Fielding's efforts the Female Orphan Asylum opened for the numerous vagrant girls in danger of being forced into prostitution as young as 12 years of age. For seven years the girls learnt domestic arts in the Asylum and were then placed in households. Later, the Magdalen Hospital—'a Public Place of Reception for Penitent Prostitutes'—gave domestic training to older girls. Fielding hoped to reduce crime by removing youngsters from evil surroundings and by reforming delinquents. These novel and humane ideas barely affected government policy

39

which continued to be one of repression and punishment well into the nineteenth century.

Charity and Sunday schools

Some eighteenth-century reformers hoped to reduce crime by giving slum children a religious education. They hoped these youngsters would be converted to virtuous law-abiding and, very important, hard-working citizens by learning to read the Bible and recite the Catechism. The Society for Promoting Christian Knowledge (founded 1698) established over 2,000 charity schools with these objects in mind, but most poor children could not attend: they had to work because their scanty earnings were needed by their parents. Infants often attended village dame schools where they 'tumbled over one another like puppies in a kennel', learnt little more than the alphabet and left as soon as they could earn a wage.

However, Sunday was a free day for all children. Robert Raikes was disturbed by the hooliganism of neglected children in Gloucester on that day each week

25 Unruly behaviour at a village dame school. At such schools there was usually more play than work, and generally only the rudiments of education were taught.

26 'Ragged' children at John Pound's shop in Portsmouth, which opened in 1818. This marked the beginning of the Ragged School movement which made evening schools available for poor, neglected children who had no other opportunity for education.

and so he set up the first Sunday school there in 1780. Success led to similar attempts elsewhere. In 1785 William Fox set up the London Society for the Establishment of Sunday Schools and within ten years 250,000 were attending each week. But one day in seven was not enough and the lessons were forgotten before the next week. Hence schemes began for full-time education and evening schools. From 1811 the National Society for Promoting the Education of the Children of the Poor in the Principles of the Established Church opened day schools, as did the nonconformist British and Foreign School Society from 1814.

In 1818 John Pounds, a Portsmouth shoemaker, opened his shop in the evenings to any neglected children who wished to learn something. Nineteen years later the London City Mission followed suit and opened five evening schools for children too ragged and verminous to be allowed into any other schools. During the next 30 years the ragged school movement flourished in the slum areas of large towns and from 1844 was under the guidance of the Ragged School Union.

Ragged schools, refuges and orphanages

They certainly had plenty of customers. In 1850 there were an estimated '30,000 destitute, filthy, lawless children in London alone, the source of nineteen-twentieths of the crime committed'. Fifteen years later a survey of certain districts of Manchester showed that for every 15 children between the ages of three and 12, one was at work, six at school and the other eight were neglected. 'And what are

27 This drawing shows the dining-hall of the orphanage at Erdington in 1869. During Queen Victoria's reign, men like Dr Barnado and Lord Shaftesbury set up voluntary organizations and homes to help the ever-growing number of homeless children.

these children doing if they are not at school? They are idling in the streets and wynds; tumbling about in the gutters; selling matches; running errands; working in tobacco shops, cared for by no man.'

Meanwhile poor law officials protested that they were already so overburdened by pauper children in their care that they could not afford to search out and help vagabond youngsters. In 1803 the official number of permanent child paupers was 195,000 and this excluded the wandering, homeless youngsters. In 1837 alone, 39,371 unwanted babies were born. The mortality rate of foundlings in Dublin was over 50 per cent during the 1830s.

Wealthy Victorians became determined to provide shelter for the thousands of homeless children through voluntary organisations since the government seemed either unable or unwilling to take the responsibility. Teachers in ragged schools had noticed that many children had no home to return to when the classes ended for the night and so the movement branched out to provide night refuges. The first House of Refuge for Boys had opened at Glasgow in 1837. London got its first in

1846, followed by the Grotto Passage Refuge in Marylebone, the Field Lane Night Refuge and many more. From these experiments grew the National Refuges for the Homeless and Destitute Children, now known as the Shaftesbury Homes.

Other famous voluntary agencies which struggled to help the huge numbers of homeless children were the Church of England's Society for Waifs and Strays and Dr Barnardo's homes. The doctor opened his first home in Commerical Road, Stepney, in 1867, and soon the motto over the door of every Barnardo home read 'No Child Ever Turned Away'. Before he died in 1905 over 100 homes had been opened and a total of 60,000 children cared for.

Besides these societies to help orphan children there were voluntary societies which campaigned for the better protection of infants in workhouses and in families with working mothers. These women usually left their babies with day-nurses—old ladies who quietened their charges with Godfrey's Cordial or Mrs Wilkinson's Soothing Syrup. Due to these concoctions of opium and treacle 'great numbers of infants perish, either suddenly from an overdose, or, as more commonly happens, slowly, painfully and insidiously'. Other infants died from being fed heavy paps containing tough, poor food. Girls of seven and eight were often

Infant protection

28 The playroom of a London crèche in 1871. Mothers could leave their children in these crèches (day nurseries) and then go on to their own jobs.

paid to 'mind' infants and consequently some of the infants died from neglect or misguided treatment.

In the later nineteenth century crèches (day nurseries) opened in most large towns where working mothers could leave infants for only a small fee to cover the food. A clause in the Factory and Workshops Act of 1891 prohibited employers from employing a woman within four weeks of her confinement. But this only meant a possibly disastrous loss of earnings and the real answer only came in 1911 when the government first instituted a scheme of maternity benefits.

The Society for the Protection of Infant Life pressed the government to regulate the activities of baby-farmers who were paid to look after pauper children. The Infant Life Protection Act of 1872 required baby-farmers to register with the local authority and obtain a licence. Also, an infant's death had to be reported and a doctor's certificate produced. However, these terms were widely ignored and the business continued to be profitable and the babies' death-rate high.

Public pressure and government action

It was persistent agitation by individuals and voluntary societies which had forced a rather reluctant government to pass this act for the protection of infant life. Equally lengthy pressure was needed before the government would change the system for dealing with young law-breakers. In 1844 children received much the same punishments as adults and one in every 304 children between the ages of

29 Dinner is served at Tothill Boys' Prison. The boys also spent all day in this room engaged on the monotonous job of shredding strands of old rope, a task known as oakum picking.

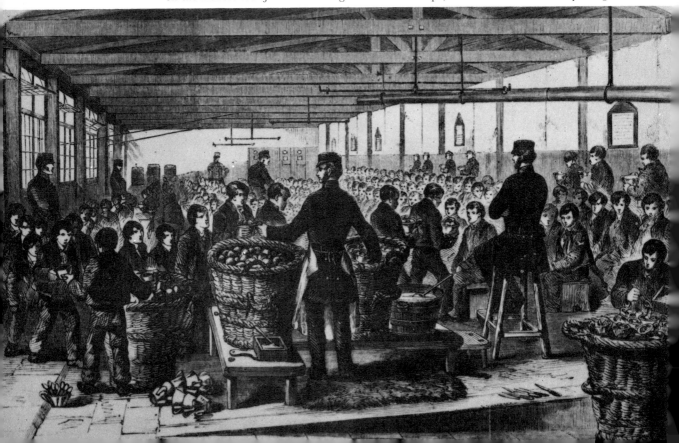

30 A London school board man unearths homeless boys at half-past two in the morning in 1871. Tomorrow they will be made to attend school.

10 and 20 was in prison, mixing freely with adult criminals. There was prolonged agitation for the special treatment of delinquents with separation from adult offenders and emphasis on reform and not punishment.

The first separate prison for boys was built at Parkhurst in 1838 and in 1854 the government was persuaded to pass a Reformatory Schools Act. The schools subsequently set up were the forerunners of our modern approved schools. Pleas for probation and not imprisonment for children had begun as early as 1827 but it was 60 years before the government passed the Probation of First Offenders Act, which enabled the delinquent to be helped instead of being labelled as criminal.

Victorian educationalists also had to fight hard before a state system of education was established by Forster's Education Act of 1870. School boards for each area were to build elementary schools where adequate ones did not already exist, so that every child in the country would be within reach of a school. The Elementary Education Act of 1876 made compulsory education universal: every parent had to ensure that his child received sufficient elementary education, that is, could read, write and do arithmetic adequately.

At last most children began to receive full-time education. However, as the urchins emerged from the obscurity of the slums, the general public was able to see for the first time that many were physically neglected. In 1889, 50,000 London school-board children were recorded as being under-fed: 'Puny, pale-faced,

31 A rush of poor children for free dinners at the King Edward's Mission, Whitechapel, in 1890. These free meals were another example of the way the voluntary societies were doing all they could to help the poor, the sick and the destitute.

scantily-clad and badly shod, these small and feeble folk may be found sitting limp and chill on the school benches in all the poorer parts of London.'

Once again voluntary societies were the first to extend help to these unhealthy slum children and in the 1880s and 1890s it became quite fashionable for the wealthy to help in these societies. The Fresh Air Fund and the Children's Country Holiday Fund took sickly youngsters for holidays. Other societies supplied cheap or free meals. For example, the Destitute Children's Dinner Society dispensed 290,476 dinners at 55 dining-rooms in London during 1891. The Children's Happy Evenings Association attempted to keep children off the streets by organising games and giving moral instruction. The Salvation Army and Boys' Brigade hoped to use military discipline and uniform to improve the bearing and manners of slum lads. In the larger towns, there were Homes for Working Boys, for those who could not afford lodgings. The Metropolitan Association for Befriending Young Servants, the Girls' Friendly Society and the Ladies Association for the Care of Friendless Girls were each ready with advice and help for servant girls.

In the 1880s many societies combined with the Society for the Prevention of Cruelty to Children, which had begun in a small way at Liverpool in 1882. The Society fought to alter the contemporary view that a child was its parents' private property and that the state had no right to interfere. Through the Society's efforts the Children's Charter Act was passed in 1889. Neglect or ill-treatment of children became a crime with heavy penalties, married women could give evidence against their husbands, permits would be granted to search houses where ill-treatment was suspected and children could be taken out of the custody of persons judged to be unfit to care for them.

W. E. Gladstone, a Victorian Prime Minister, had once said that whatever efforts the government made, the answer to 'the question whether the English father is to be the father of a happy family and the centre of a united home . . . must depend on himself'. However, by the dawn of the twentieth century reformers had forced society to recognise that the British child's education, health, protection and contentment fell on the shoulders of the state and not just the father. Because of state help the twentieth-century child was destined to lead a much happier life.

Further Reading
Charles Dickens, *Oliver Twist*
        Nicholas Nickleby
C. S. Montague, *Sixty Years in Waifdom. The Ragged School Movement*
Gladstone Purves, *Mudlarks and Ragged Schools*
Margaret Hewitt, *Wives and Mothers in Victorian Industry*
Frances Hopkirk, *Nobody Wanted Sam*—the story of the unwelcomed child in England 1530–1848.

5 Child Workers 1700–1900

The sufferings of nineteenth-century factory children were well publicised by a series of Commissioners' reports on various industries. Yet terrible conditions did not arrive with the Industrial Revolution. For centuries children had been exploited as cheap labour, but no one had been shocked enough to start investigations.

Most eighteenth-century folk thought it beneficial for working-class children to commence work as young as possible. In 1697 John Locke advised the Board of Trade that the problem of poverty and poor relief would be eased if little ones over three were taught to earn their living at working schools for spinning. Rich folk felt that to find employment for a young child was an act of kindness and assistance to himself and his family. On his travels Daniel Defoe was delighted to find most Yorkshire children over four at work and that at Taunton all except a few neglected children could earn their own living from five years of age. Later in the century, an American visitor voiced two arguments in favour of child labour: 'Employment not only keeps their little minds from vice but . . . takes a heavy burden from their

32 Country children of the nineteenth century – the boy is employed as a bird-scarer, and a young girl is looking after toddlers.

poor parents.' In a speech in 1796 William Pitt referred to the contribution child workers made to the country's wealth. However, a rather more experienced and disillusioned old man observed that 'the creatures were set to work as soon as they could crawl and their parents were the hardest task-masters'.

Cottage industry

Unless children lived in an area of village industry, they did outdoor farm work for their parents. The youngest were bird-scarers, goose girls and shepherd lads, or else weeded and picked stones in the fields. There was little respite during winter when boys learnt to plait straw for horses' collars, to stuff the sheep-skins used as cart-saddles and to carve wooden kitchen utensils.

At least there was fresh air and seasonal variation in their work, whereas the children of cottage industries faced the same dreary routine throughout the year. In the home woollen industry the boys carded the wool, the wife and daughters spun it and the man's task was weaving. Alternatively, the wife received wool from a large manufacturer and earned ninepence a day for carding and spinning the wool and elder daughters fourpence a day for their help. The younger children frequently worked for a neighbouring weaver winding thread on to bobbins for him. Midlands children did regular hours from five years of age in lace, glove, button-making, knitting and embroidery industries. They generally attended cottage schools owned by the mistress or by a dealer who provided materials and employed a teacher or overlooker to supervise. Though called schools they were just workshops.

Pauper apprentices

Poor law authorities established workhouses throughout the eighteenth century to occupy the unfortunate pauper or destitute children. The workhouse movement had begun towards the end of the previous century when it was argued that 'the young should be inured to labour' and should learn to keep themselves. By 1770 a government survey revealed that young paupers spent their days on unskilled tasks like spinning, knitting, sewing and pin-making. Then they were apprenticed as young as possible in unskilled trades which required cheap drudges.

The unluckiest mites were sold for a few guineas to chimney-sweeps. They were forced to crawl the narrow, suffocating chimney passages to clear accumulations of soot. At first they would be terror-stricken by the dark and by the choking soot, and would suffer painful sores on elbows, feet and knees until their skin eventually hardened. Some lads were never washed; many developed a disease known as chimney-sweeps' cancer; most were stunted in growth and 'knapped kneed' through climbing when their bones were soft; and all ran the continual danger of suffocation and burning.

From the 1760s thousands of paupers were dispatched to the recently-built northern cotton mills. Machinery was slowly replacing the work of human hands in many industries, creating jobs which required neither intelligence nor strength. This gave child labour a commercial value hitherto unknown. London poor law authorities were delighted to hand over their youngsters to the mill-owners and so

49

be rid of a drain on funds and get a payment for each child into the bargain. The wretched pauper mill-workers lived in 'prentice-houses and their labouring hours were limited only by utter exhaustion.

The mills   In the nineteenth century mills began to switch from the use of water to steam power and hence, instead of being located alongside remote streams, mills could now be built in towns where neighbourhood children could be taken on instead of imported paupers. At first many parents refused to allow their children to enter the mills. But soon competition and hardship forced them to change. For instance, the hand-loom weaver lost custom to the factories, the family's wages fell and there was little home employment for the children. Parish relief was refused to a weaver with children who could be sent to the mill, hence his children commenced work at the mill, usually at six or seven years of age. Their day began at 6 a.m. and ended at 7 or 8 p.m., with a 20-hour day at busy times. Three-quarters of the children worked as piecers, that is they knotted together threads broken in the various roving and spinning machines. Others picked up bits of material or replaced bobbins. One factory owner's investigations revealed that a piecer walked 20 miles in 12 hours of work.

So exhausting was the employment that only brutality could keep the children awake. A Leeds mill worker told a committee of enquiry in 1832 that the overseers 'would tap them over the head, or nip them over the nose or give them a pinch of snuff, or throw water in their faces, or pull them off where they were and job them about to keep them waking'. These overseers wielded either heavy iron sticks called billy-rollers or heavy leather thongs. Some children returned home too tired to eat their supper or to remove their clothes at night and one factory worker reported: 'I have seen them fall asleep and they have been performing their work with their hands while they were asleep, after the billy had stopped, when their work was over.'

Cheap labour was in constant demand, children sometimes worked when their parents could not find employment, and families came to depend on their meagre

34 Factory children too exhausted for Sunday School on their only free day of the week.

earnings. The work in most mechanised industries was more physically dangerous and mentally exhausting than had been the jobs of pre-industrial times. Now children had the responsibility of being their own masters and not just assistants. Long hours, wearying tasks and poor food combined seriously to damage their bodily health. They were pale, delicate, sickly children stunted in growth, with many suffering from curvature and distortion of the spine, or deformity of the limbs and lung diseases. Many died from consumption or atrophy (wasting away through undernourishment). Needless to say a very small proportion indeed were able to read or had any schooling.

Ineffective action
The Health and Morals of Apprentices Act of 1802 had limited the pauper children's hours to 12 a day and insisted on the provision of education. The act did not apply to other child slaves and anyway was ignored since no inspectors were appointed to enforce the clauses. Attempts to introduce further legislation met fierce opposition in Parliament. Factory-owners argued that 'nothing is more favourable to morals than habits of early subordination, industry and regularity'. They warned that a shortening of hours would increase costs, prevent industries from matching foreign competition and, in any case, was an unwarrantable interference with private property.

Yet Parliament did pass an act in 1819 which limited the labour of children over nine in cotton factories to 12 hours daily and forbade altogether the employment of those under nine. But again no inspectors were appointed and so the act proved ineffective. In 1832 Sadler's committee made detailed enquiries into the conditions of child workers. Its horrific report aided the passage of the Factory Act of 1833 which did provide for inspectors. By this act, children under nine were forbidden to work in all textile mills except silk; those under 13 were limited to nine hours daily or 48 in a week; and 12 hours was the daily maximum for those under 18. Even this act was evaded since the children worked by relays and inspectors could not know at what time any group had started.

An influential section of the public was now aware that conditions of child labour in many industries were deplorable and agitation in Parliament by Lord Ashley (later the Earl of Shaftesbury) and John Fielden led to commissions of enquiry which reported to Parliament during the next 30 years. The first report by the Commission on the Employment of Children in 1842 revealed such ghastly conditions in the mines that the Mines and Collieries Regulation Bill became law in the same year.

The mines
Mine workers began as young as five or six as trappers. They opened and shut doors which controlled the draught of air through the mines, and they barely saw the light of day during the winter months, except on Sunday, their day off. When older, they worked as fillers, loading the carriages with hewn coal at the face, or as 'hurriers'—dragging or pushing the carriages from the face to the foot of the shaft. In the very small seams they had to crawl with the load tied to one of their feet.

35 A girl 'hurrier'. This poor child dragged or pushed the trucks of coal from the foot of the shaft to the coal face, through a tunnel less than two feet high. This drawing was one of several in an official report on child labour in the mines of 1842, which shocked the nation into realizing that such conditions should not be allowed to prevail.

36 A sketch of 1871 shows a watch boy in the deep, muddy, gloomy tunnel that led to a coal face.

37 Two pictures of the brickmaking trade in the nineteenth century. The one above shows children carrying the clay; their clothes are tattered, they have no shoes. The work is hard and tedious, the pay poor. When pay does come, as in the picture below, they are too weary to be excited.

They finished the day, 'with their arms and knees streaming with blood and the knees looking as if the caps had been pulled off'.

Their elder sisters carried the coal up ladders to the surface in baskets strapped to their backs. Serious accidents were frequent: girls fell from the ladders, gases exploded and the winding machinery to bring the youngsters to the surface occasionally broke. Coal dust irreparably harmed eyesight, lungs and skin, and, as in the factories, children had to be terrorized to force more work from them. The act of 1842 stopped boys under 10 and all females from working underground. However, subsequent reform was so slow that the minimum age for boys working underground was not raised to 12 years till 1887.

The next report of the Children's Employment Commission in 1843 revealed *Workshop trades* that conditions were generally worse in small rather than large factories and worse still in workshops where trades operated on a small scale. The report did enable Lord Ashley and John Fielden to secure the passage of a bill in 1847 which limited all textile and mine workers under 18 to a 10-hour day. But youngsters in other trades remained unprotected. In 1861, Ashley (now the Earl of Shaftesbury) secured a general commission of inquiry into the employment of children in trades and manufactures. The Commission investigated for five years and turned in a horrific catalogue of child abuse.

Children in the pottery trade worked very irregular hours in temperatures between 100° and 120°. In winter masters sent them out into freezing temperatures to do errands, wearing no stockings, shoes or jackets. Not surprisingly, many died of consumption and asthma. One boy of 12 regularly arrived home from work at 8 or 9 p.m.: 'I am very tired when I get home a-nights. Get my supper, and go to bed and up again at ha'f past foive.' George Smith, a boy of nine in the brick-making trade, carried 40 pound loads of clay throughout a 13-hour day. Children employed in heading pins and nails were beaten with horse-whips, files or straps if caught relaxing by the woman who patrolled their ranks.

In the small workshop trades the work itself was not injurious but the hours were long. Youngsters in the misnamed schools of pillow-making, straw-plaiting and card-setting generally did a 12-hour day, with sometimes a 16- or 18-hour day. Weavers' assistants in the Kidderminster carpet trade endured long hours and Sunday work to complete the weekly quota, as did helpers in the fustian-cutting trade.

At many dressmaking establishments the shorter winter hours were 8 a.m. till 11 p.m. Girls did not stand the strain for long. If they did not leave to marry or find other work, their health broke and they usually died of consumption. Meanwhile replacements of fresh country girls had arrived. Young bobbin lace-makers had to sit for hours bent double over their cushions. Their ribs eventually became displaced, leading to early death. Conditions were often worst when children worked for their parents. A girl glove-maker's comments illustrate this:

Little children are kept up shamefully late if there is work, especially on   55

Thursday and Friday nights, when it is often till 11 or 12. They have to make two days out of Friday. Mothers will pin them to their knee to keep them to their work and, if they are sleepy, give them a slap on the head to keep them awake. If the children are pinned up so, they cannot fall when they are slapped or when they go to sleep. . . . The child has so many fingers set for it to stitch before it goes to bed and must do them.

Change of heart   Traditional attitudes to child labour were changed by the commissioners' appalling reports, by increasing humane concern for child welfare and by new economic arguments. For example, manufacturers found that work completed at the end of a hard day was defective or spoiled and meant loss, not profit. Furthermore, unhealthy children meant a weak adult labour force in the future. Doctors pointed out that in the pottery industry 'each successive generation of potters becomes more dwarfed and less robust than the preceding one'. Fears that the factory acts would ruin the cotton industry had proved groundless. Textile manufacturers now thought it equitable that inspection and regulation should be extended to other industries besides their own.

Between 1845 and 1861 the factory laws were extended to industries allied to textiles. In 1864, following the report of the Childrens' Employment Commission, which had begun investigations three years earlier, the paper-staining, match-

38 A London military tailor and his family in 1863. Pay was so poor in this trade that the youngsters had to work extremely long hours, and continual close work resulted in blindness for many before they became adults.

39 Many vagrant children found some form of employment on the streets of the large towns. Here we see a well-to-do gentleman about to reward a young crossing-sweeper.

'Shoes 'vell polished' shows another gainful form of employment – although the boys look almost too immaculate to be true.

making, pottery and cartridge-making industries were dealt with. Further commission reports led to the Factory Acts Extensions Act and the Workshops Regulation Act of 1867 which between them brought protection to children in small workshops and even home industry. Lastly, in 1875, came the first effective act to prohibit the use of boy chimney-sweeps. Adult sweeps were prohibited from business unless they had a licence, which was renewed annually and could be refused if they employed boys.

The legislation of the previous half century was drawn together by the Consolidation Act of 1878: no child under eight was to be employed in any craft, children under 12 could work only on a half-time system, and maximum daily hours for young persons were 12 hours with $1\frac{1}{2}$ hours included for meal-times. Finally, children had to attend school for at least 10 hours weekly.

• In 1876 full-time attendance at school became compulsory for all up to 10 years of age, though school board officials had an extremely difficult task to track down the thousands of truant and vagrant children or those kept from school to work for their parents. Every town still had its 'street arabs' and its pickpockets. 'Mudlarks' still scurried out on to the River Thames mud at low tide to search for scrap to sell for pennies. 'Toshers' still combed the sewers. Boys and girls hawked wares in the streets from baskets and barrows, and others were always at hand to open cab-doors or hold a gentleman's horses.

You could still see some of them even after an act of 1891 prohibited full-time employment until the age of 11. This act represents the peak of Victorian child labour legislation—a rather modest achievement after a century of agitation by humanitarians.

Further Reading
Frances Trollope, *Michael Armstrong*
Mrs Gaskell, *Mary Barton*
Royston Pike, *Human Documents of the Industrial Revolution*
Olive Dunlop, *English Apprenticeship and Child Labour*

6 Fortunate Victorians

Childhood barely existed for most British children at the end of the eighteenth century, since they began a lifetime of labour as soon as they were capable of simple tasks. By contrast, the fortunate children of the wealthy classes generally enjoyed sympathetic treatment and special provision for the needs of a lengthy childhood.

Most middle- and upper-class families had well-equipped nurseries with their attendant maids to cater for all the child's needs. Unfortunately, contact between parents and their offspring was still not very close. The youngsters spent most of the time under the charge of the nurse or governess. Certainly the mother visited the nursery frequently and children had lunch with mother and her guests, but father often returned from work after their bed-time and saw little of his children. Sir Osbert Sitwell argued that the nursery and nurses existed to keep the children out of sight: 'Parents were aware that the child would be a nuisance and a whole bevy of servants, in addition to the complex guardianship of nursery and school-

Methods of upbringing

40 Most middle- and upper-class families employed nurses to look after their children, so it was very important to select the conscientious, attentive kind of nurse shown here.

room, was necessary not so much to aid the infant as to screen him from his father and mother, except on such occasions as he could be used by them as adjuncts, toys or decoration.' This description applied only to a minority of parents; most provided a nursery and maids to ensure the physical well-being of their child and regarded it as the ideal place for their offspring to learn how to live and behave.

The French philosopher Rousseau's recent ideas on child-rearing influenced some parents. He argued that nurses and parents should appeal to the child's reason instead of instilling adult behaviour by continual beatings as punishment for faults. He wished the child to learn by experience, not blind obedience, so he should be told why he ought to act in a particular way. If he did not listen then he should be left to learn by painful experience.

The theory contained many faults and dangers. We now realise that a child is too unprotected and helpless to learn just by experience. Guidance is needed otherwise accidents occur. It was not realised in nineteenth-century society that a child cannot act and think rationally, his mind and attitude to life being completely different to that of an adult. However, Rousseau's theories did at least reject accepted notions of beating behaviour into children and instead encouraged a gentler approach.

Two other pioneers of child-rearing methods abroad were Friedrich Froebel and Johann Pestalozzi. The latter devised a form of education based on learning by direct observation rather than the rote learning of a dull catalogue of facts. In 1837 Friedrich Froebel opened his first kindergarten in Germany. Harshness and rigidity of teaching were replaced by greater freedom for the child and the excitement of discovery.

41 An advertisement of 1897 which shows the popular style of prams for the well-to-do.

Unfortunately these theories were only taken up by a minority of Victorians: for most youngsters upbringing was still strict. Life in the nursery operated with clockwork regularity: breakfast at 8, dinner at 12, tea at 6. As they grew older children joined mother for luncheon at 1 o'clock and spent an hour before dinner in her dressing-room. If their mother made 'morning calls' they might be taken out with her as a treat, though they had to remain in the carriage whilst she visited. Usually, however, the afternoon meant a walk in the park with nanny or dancing lessons to learn the polka and waltz.

Nursery food was very plain. Porridge, bread and milk always appeared for breakfast. The usual midday fare was turnips, cauliflowers or cabbage, potatoes and boiled mutton for the main course, followed by rice pudding. Fresh fruit was ruled out, as were puff pastries and confectionery and drinks of tea and coffee. A stick of sugar-candy was a real treat and sweets were uncommon. Even by the 1870s menus had improved little in variety, though eggs, stewed fruit, sponge cake and biscuits had been added.

Children not only had to endure unappetizing food: worse still they suffered unpleasant remedies or preventives for illness. In the first half of the century infectious diseases and fevers were still common, with epidemics of typhus, small-pox and cholera, though later that century medical science succeeded in control-

42 A little boy with his nursery rocking horse in 1874.

43 Typical dresses and hats for girls in 1889.

ling many epidemic diseases of childhood. Many infants died from croup, a form of asthma, and from convulsions.

Nurseries were scrubbed clean of dirt and children had to undergo the daily terror of the cold morning tub and the scrubbing and soap of the Saturday evening bath. The nursery medicine cupboard held syrup of senna, rhubarb, liquorice, treacle, brimstone, Dr Gregory's powder, tar water, cinnamon, blackberry syrup for coughs and blackcurrant tea for colds. A purgative was given every Friday night and any sign of resistance was met with by an immediate dose of castor oil. Altogether there was far too much dosing. Another misconception was the fear of fresh air. Except in warm weather the nursery windows remained shut, children stayed in when the weather was cold and wet and, when they were allowed out, were ridiculously muffled up and overburdened with clothes.

Clothes   For most of the century children had to wear most impractical and cumbersome clothes. Fashions had been sensible at the beginning of the nineteenth century. Boys had loose, light-coloured clothes with open-necked shirts. Girls wore dainty, muslin or gauze frocks, with no constrictions around the waist. Unfortunately by 1825 filmy fabrics were being replaced by heavier materials, fuller skirts, puffed sleeves, long and noticeable drawers or pantalettes and elaborate trimmings. Even hats became larger and overburdened with flowers and ribbons. Soon girls were wearing four or five stiffly starched, corded petticoats to hold out their skirts.

Boys' clothes had become tighter and less comfortable and were quite inadequate for playing. By 1850 the crinoline, a sort of flexible wire cage worn under the dress, had replaced the petticoats and made many little girls look like walking mushrooms. Frilly, open-ended drawers were worn and, as the writer Frederic Roe has observed, little girls were frequently warned of their gradual descent by the shout of a passing urchin 'Maud-ee, yerdrorsercomindahn' or the nanny's whisper 'Lilian, dear, you are *showing*'.

In the 1870s boys had to wear tight jackets, stiff Eton collars and hard-rimmed toppers, though towards the end of the century they wore the more pleasant sailor suits and reefer coats. For girls the bustle replaced the crinoline and was even less practical because the cloth was pulled back tightly over the hips to bunch it up at the back and the wearer could barely move. Worse still, with the bustle you needed a narrow waist and girls sometimes injured themselves and often fainted at school because they wore excessive tightlacing to achieve an 18-inch waist.

Parents insisted on dressing their daughters as dolls for family prestige, to keep in fashion and because little girls were expected to be dignified and decorative not active and romping. Elder sisters accepted the burdens of fashion because the only real career open to early Victorians was to attract an eligible young man and get married.

Georgian views of the nature of a girl's education persisted in the first half of the nineteenth century. A girl should not learn debasing domestic tasks but train to be an accomplished and well-bred lady. She did not need an academic education since she would never have to earn her living and anyway girls were not considered to have sufficient brain-power for rigorous study. Every nice girl would learn the accomplishments of music, singing, dancing, drawing and deportment, which would increase her chances in the marriage market.

Education

By 1870 feminine demureness and propriety were less favoured and soon women began to make social and economic claims. Before there had been very few careers open and girls merely helped at home before marriage. Earlier in the century some enlightened parents had sent their daughters to private schools, such as Roedean and Cheltenham Ladies College. The purpose of these schools was not profit but the provision of education in 'modern subjects'. Many girls' boarding schools opened in the 1850s and attracted mainly the middle classes.

Already boarding education had become very popular for boys, a trend helped by the cheapness and speed of rail travel. Private schools for the middle classes were profit-making institutions supplying what the customer wanted—usually a vocational training and a good social background. Dr Arnold of Rugby explained the aims of the even more popular public schools: 'What we look for . . . is first religious and moral principles; secondly gentlemanly conduct; thirdly intellectual ability.'

Technical and vocational education had become the main route to success for the middle classes. Many parents felt that the fewer children they had the better educational opportunities they could afford for them. This is one explanation for the noticeable fall in the birth-rate and the smaller families from 1850. Also, women were engaging in more activities outside the home and wanted to be freer from home ties. In addition, children were costing more because more of them survived to adulthood, since improved sanitation and the advances in medical science had cut the infant death-rate. Finally, domestic assistance—nursery maids, governesses and servants—were now costing more.

Smaller families meant greater attention for the child and a more intimate family group. Even better, by mid-century wealthy parents had adopted a much kindlier attitude towards their children's upbringing and now believed their off-spring could become intelligent, sensible adults without being beaten and frightened; children were encouraged to enjoy themselves and to play. The increasing variety and number of children's toys, parlour and outdoor games, hobbies, books, magazines and comics are proof of sympathetic parental attitudes. Nursery infants had rocking-horses, toy soldiers, wax dolls (which could open and shut their eyes and say 'Mamma'), Jack-in-the-box, monkeys on a stick, building bricks and so on.

Recreations

Until the 1880s perhaps the most popular indoor pastime for children who had left the nursery was the toy theatre. Stages could be bought ready-made and actors and scenery printed on sheets of paper or card—penny plain and twopence coloured—could be cut out and slid on and off the stage by attached wires. Educational hobbies were encouraged, particularly the collecting of shells, wild-flowers for pressing, birds' eggs, butterflies and stamps (after 1840), while young

44 A Victorian middle-class family. By then there was more affection and contact between parents and children, who were encouraged to read, play games and generally enjoy themselves.

45 A little girl playing with her dolls' house in 1898.

46 Pollock's toy shop in Hoxton Road at the end of the nineteenth century, showing a toy theatre and on the shelves behind, 'penny plains' and 'twopenny coloureds'. This shop still exists as a toy museum.

ladies filled scrapbooks with cuttings and pictures from magazines. Fathers tried to teach the laws of nature with scientific toys like the magic lantern, the kaleidoscope, the zoëtrope and mechanical toys powered by clockwork, gravity, spinning fly-wheels and steam. Even pea-shooters were sold as scientific toys: they demonstrated the principles of compressed air!

There was a tremendous growth in juvenile literature. English fairy-stories regained popularity, Hans Andersen's tales were translated in 1846, Edward Lear published his *Book of Nonsense* and later came Lewis Carroll's *Alice in Wonderland* and Kingsley's *Water Babies*. Older children revelled in adventure stories specially written for them by Captain Marryat (*Children of the New Forest*), R. Ballantyne (*Coral Island*), R. L. Stevenson (*Treasure Island*) and G. A. Henty.

In the later nineteenth century magazines flooded the market. The first nursery magazine was *The Monthly Packet*, published in 1851, and later *Aunt Judy's Magazine*. Elder brothers were thrilled 'by wild and wonderful but healthy fiction' in *Boy's Own Paper*, *Boy's Own Magazine*, *Boys of England* and *Chums*. Working-class children could enjoy 'penny dreadfuls', 'bloods' and comics featuring Dick Turpin, Robin Hood, Buffalo Bill and, later, the detective Sexton Blake. Wealthy parents no doubt frowned to find their children enjoyed the popular comics like *Chips* and *Comic Cuts* which first appeared in 1890.

Wealthy and poor children alike enjoyed simple games with hoops, marbles, tiddly-winks, diabolo, peg-tops and rubber balls. Poorer children could not afford the more expensive toys we have already mentioned. They did not enjoy the comforts of a nursery, the attentions of a nurse-maid or the luxury of a wholesome diet. But during the twentieth century the gap between fortunate and underprivileged youngsters narrowed considerably and most children came to share roughly the same welfare, education and recreational facilities.

Further Reading
Jane Austen, *Pride and Prejudice*
Marion Lochhead, *Young Victorians*
      Their First Ten Years
F. Gordon Roe, *The Victorian Child*
Mary Gibbs, *The Years of the Nannies*

7 The Century of the Child

Some writers in 1900 hailed the new era as 'The Century of the Child'. It is doubtful whether this enthusiasm was shared by the one-third of British families who lived below the poverty line: their children were still battling for existence. Over half the children of London's East End died before they were five, and a third of all workhouse children died in their first year of life. All this at a time when the numbers of infant deaths were falling spectacularly for the country as a whole.

Slum children were born in dangerous, insanitary conditions since parents could not afford the 5s charged by the cheapest midwives and it was most unlikely that expectant mothers would be admitted to hospital. Mothers were too ill or undernourished to be able to breast-feed their children and instead used skimmed milk, ignoring the labels which said it was unsuitable for infants. Still poorer families could afford to use only flour and water.

If these children survived infancy they usually showed early signs of malnutrition because of their inadequate diet. A report on schoolchildren in 1907 spoke of enormous numbers with bad teeth, poor eyesight and hearing, ringworm, scabies, scurvy, deformities due to rickets and heads scratched raw through lice. Social workers begged the government to provide crèches, day-nurseries, clinics and school dinners, while teachers pointed out the impossibility of educating children who were underfed and diseased.

Eventually the government recognised the necessity for making medical and nutritional services a part of the education system. In 1906 local authorities were given permission and grants to provide a school meals service, though some areas were slow to take up the offer. School medical inspection was already common: now it was made compulsory, and also the first school dental clinics opened. But there was little use in medical examination of schoolchildren when the damage to the child had already been done in infancy. Eventually the Maternity and Child Welfare Act of 1918 gave local authorities powers to 'make arrangements for safeguarding the health of mothers and of children under five'.

Children in desperate need of help were the hordes of pauper, vagrant, abandoned, illegitimate and delinquent youngsters. Many workhouse children suffered disgraceful conditions according to a Royal Commission report of 1905. For example some London workhouse children were never allowed outside. The responsibility for workhouse children's health was therefore transferred to the Ministry of Health.

The Victorians had established penalties for the ill-treatment and neglect of children in 1889, yet since then governments had left enforcement mainly to the voluntary National Society for the Prevention of Cruelty to Children. In 1907

State help for slum children

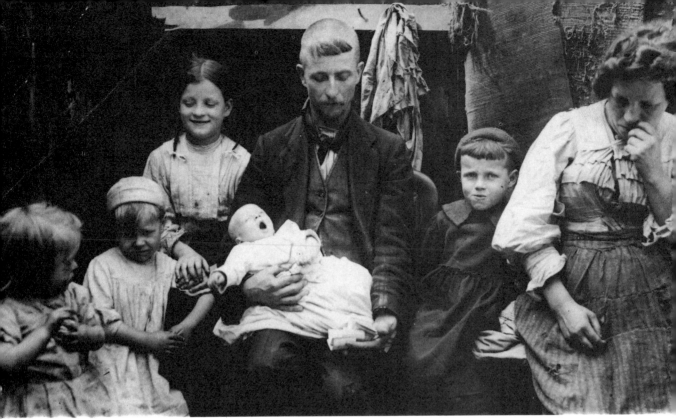

47 These two photographs illustrate the differences in dress and cleanliness between rich and poor children in the early twentieth century. In the photograph above we see a poor family of London's East End in 1912. The father holds a handful of pawn tickets and is no doubt wondering where he will find the money to feed his five children. By contrast (**below**) some youngsters of rich families were cared for extremely well. Here are some nursemaids with their charges in 1913.

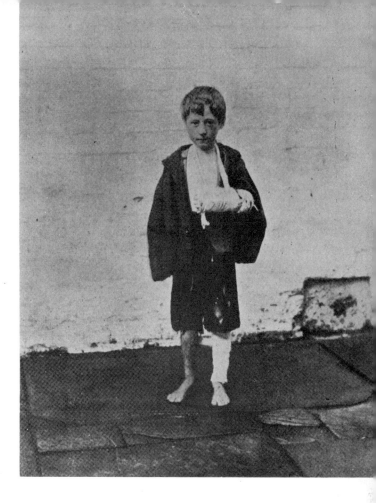

48 A victim of violent assault. The voluntary N.S.P.C.C. dealt with thousands of similar cases every year and society was at last treating parental cruelty as a criminal offence.

alone the society obtained 2,180 prosecutions but was overburdened with cases and in 1908 a Children's Act made local authorities responsible for the discovery and prosecution of neglect. They had to inspect all premises where children were minded for profit; make sure that they were notified of all deaths within 48 hours; and prosecute any parental negligence, even leaving a child in a room with an unprotected fire. Parental cruelty could now mean a five-year prison sentence, whereas only 50 years before the killing of infants had been conveniently ignored.

A revolution had also occurred in attitudes to young lawbreakers. Prolonged Victorian agitation had resulted in an act of 1887 which permitted the probation of first offenders. Now the first institution to give special attention to young offenders opened in 1902 near the village of Borstal and six years later an act of Parliament extended the Borstal system to the 16 to 21 year-old group. Also, juvenile courts were established for all under 16 and the death penalty was abolished for this same age-group. Finally imprisonment of children under 14 was prohibited.

Though the Victorians had been slow to help neglected and delinquent children, they had considerably reduced the exploitation of child labour but some abuses remained unchecked in 1900. The 'half-time' system permitted children

69

over 12 to spend half their day at school and the rest at work, usually in the factories or farming. Parliament stopped industries from using the system in 1911, though it continued in farming. All other children had to attend school till they reached 12, yet many were made to do wearying jobs outside school hours. Boys were parcel-carriers, lather-boys in barbers' shops, errand-boys, knockers-up, shoe-blacks, street hawkers. Their sisters were shop assistants, domestic helps, baby-minders and dress-makers. Tiny children sold matches or danced and sang in the streets—both an excuse for begging. It was difficult to discover exploitation, particularly when the child worked at home for his parents. However, an act of 1918 raised the school leaving age to 14 and until they reached this age children were permitted to work only two hours a day, and all under 12 were banned from employment altogether.

The School Attendance Officer wandered the streets and checked that children were not kept at home. Perhaps some children did prefer to work for their parents since school discipline was harsh, silence was enforced with a cane, often lessons were dull, formal and repetitive and classes numbered around sixty. But at least children now enjoyed opportunities for learning denied to earlier generations. Schools were now run by local authorities who could award scholarships to gifted poor children to attend secondary schools.

Games and toys   Children knew how to make up for the dullness of school-life by their endless variety of street-games in the evenings and holidays. Traffic was light and the slum streets resounded with the shouts of happy children. The writer Jack London observed that there was 'one beautiful sight in the east end'—little girls dancing as the organ grinder went his rounds. Two of the most popular games were hopscotch and the many variations of leapfrog. Ball games, like 'Queenie', 'French cricket' and 'One-Two-Three-and-a-lairy', rivalled the seasonal games of hoops, marbles, cigarette cards and tops. Everywhere the skipping-rope 'peppered' and girls chanted rhythmically about 'Sam Sam the Dirty Old Man' or 'The Farmer's in his Den'. Or they joined hand-clapping and ring or chasing games like the simple 'Tiggy', 'Relievo', 'French Touch' or 'Hark the Robbers Coming Through'. In 'Statues' and 'Pork and Greens' you had to avoid laughing at the mad antics and questions of the judges.

Most children could not afford to pay for toys and entertainment, except perhaps the magic lantern shows in the church hall and the occasional Saturday afternoon at a cinema. Dolls could be made from a rag or hank of hair, and boys bought tin models of steam-rollers, fire-engines or motor-cars from the penny bazaars. For children of wealthier parents this was a golden era for toys. Dolls were beautifully dressed and could perform all sorts of tricks. Soft toys like the golliwog and teddy bear appeared in shops and boys built 'Meccano' models, played with intricate electric, clockwork and steam toy vehicles or collected postmarks, postcards or cigarette cards. Parties were organized for the young children, with perhaps a marionette or Punch and Judy show, tea, and dancing.

49 The endless variety of children's street games helped to pass long evening hours and holidays. All these photographs were taken in the 1950s but the games were played in exactly the same way then as in the early twentieth century. On the left the children are playing a game called 'Jimmy, Jimmy Knacker', on the right the familiar hop-scotch.

50 Edwardian children of wealthy parents. The boys are dressed in sailor-suit style and one is playing with a diabolo toy.

51 The investiture of a scout. On the right is the scoutmaster; in the centre the recruit and his patrol leader; on the left the rest of the troop. The Boy Scout movement, founded by Robert Baden Powell, is still a popular organization.

Boys were dressed in sailor-suits for these occasions and girls generally wore white dresses with sashes. 'Sunday-best' clothes were a boy's velvet suit and lace collar, with silks and satins for the girl. The 'liberty bodice' was a replacement for corsets, yet many girls were still laced into corsets very young.

Older children attended boy and girl dances in the evening, where they danced a nervous two-step, Paul Jones or waltz. The girls were chaperoned and warned that they must not dance more than three times with the same young gentleman.

Children of all classes except the poorest were encouraged to join movements like the Boys' Brigade, Boy Scouts and Girl Guides. Robert Baden-Powell had written a book, *Aids to Scouting—A Manual for Soldiers*, based on his observations during the Boer War. The book emphasised self-reliance and individual initiative and was widely read by boys, so he rewrote the book as *Scouting for Boys*. In 1907 Baden-Powell took 30 boys to camp at Bournemouth and thus began the Boy Scout movement which rapidly attracted thousands, and later younger boys got their chance with the Cub movement. Popular demand led to the formation of the Girl Guides in 1910, with similar aims to scouting—self-reliance, service to the community, plus the feminine arts of homecraft and child care.

Reading had become a pleasure for all children. Poor children revelled in 'penny dreadfuls' and 'Blood and Thunders', though many of these horrific magazines were being replaced at the start of the twentieth century by strip-comics, such as *Comic Cuts*, or the adventure magazines *Marvel* and *Union Jack* for older boys. Middle- and upper-class parents bought *Boys Own Paper*, *Chatterbox*, *Captain* and *Girl's Realm* for their children. Between the wars adventure weeklies like *Champion* and *Wizard* grew more popular than the public-school stories in *Magnet* and *Gem*. Many new comics for younger children also came on to the market, among the best being *Rainbow*, *Playtime* and *Tiger Tim's Weekly*, and later *Beano* (1937), *Dandy* (1938) and *Magic* (1939).

Comics and books

For most Edwardian working-class children books were difficult to obtain. Families did not own many and free libraries did little to attract the child borrower. Few juvenile books were stocked and children could not browse among the shelves but had to choose their books from a catalogue. The Edwardian wealthy classes were able to buy their children the coloured fairy-books of Andrew Lang, the adventures of Peter Pan, Kipling's jungle books, Beatrix Potter's animal fantasies or E. Nesbit's family adventure stories about *The Railway Children* or *The Treasure Seekers*.

Most popular fictional characters of the inter-war years were Winnie the Pooh, William, Biggles and the children of Arthur Ransome's adventure books. Working-class children could enjoy these books in the 1930s both because reading standards had advanced and because public libraries had begun to open children's sections.

At the end of the first World War the government had shown renewed eagerness to provide a better education system for the nation's children, most of whom only attended elementary schools. The government raised the school leaving age to 14, suggested compulsory part-time continuation schools for young people who had left school and gave local authorities permission to establish nursery schools, special schools for backward and physically handicapped children and better recreational facilities for all. Sadly, the state was unable to find the money for most of these schemes because of an economic slump and later the trade depression of the 1930s. In 1931 a government report recommended a primary school system similar to the one we have today and an act of 1936 declared that the school leaving age would be 15 in 1939.

Health A world-wide organisation for child-welfare was formed in 1919 and called the Save the Children Fund. In 1924 the League of Nations adopted a 'Declaration of the Rights of the Child' formulated by the Fund. The Fund rapidly became a leading organisation for relief and rehabilitation and established model villages in Europe and the Balkans, schools for industrial training, homes for delinquent children and training hospitals.

In England school medical inspections in the early 1930s showed that nearly a quarter of elementary school-children still suffered from malnutrition, and even more had defective eyesight, tonsils and adenoids. Subsidised school milk was introduced in 1934 and by 1936 two million children were drinking school milk at their parents' cost and half a million received it free. Furthermore the thirties saw local authorities improving maternity and infant welfare schemes. By 1939 the range of social security provisions gave some help to families which lost their wage-earner through illness or unemployment, thus reducing the chance of the family's children being underfed. Also, national campaigns for the control of tuberculosis and for immunization against diphtheria helped save many young lives.

Many young people improved their health and fitness by their own efforts during the inter-war years. They sought fresh air and adventure in the suddenly popular activities of cycling, camping and hiking and were helped by the Youth Hostels Association which was started in 1930 and was part of an international movement, the Camping Club, Ramblers' Association and the Cyclists' Touring Club.

By 1939 government reforms to improve the bodily health of the nation's children had produced noticeable results. The average height and weight of schoolchildren had increased and nutritional diseases were becoming rarer. Welfare assistance was concentrating on maternity and infant benefits and law courts showed a new concern for the quality of home life of the problem child.

War children Quite suddenly all this achievement seemed in jeopardy when England declared war on Germany in September 1939. School work was interrupted, juvenile delinquency rose (partly because of the absence of so many fathers on war service), and children suffered parental deprivation because of evacuation and, later, bombing.

52 Evacuation of school children, September 1939. Labels are attached to them before they board the trains for the safety of the countryside.

Plans for evacuation from dangerous areas had been made beforehand and two days before the outbreak of the war a vast dispersal of families began. Within a few days three-quarters of a million children left 40 highly populated areas for the countryside. The months passed without air-raids and many returned. When heavy bombing began in September 1940 there was a second mass evacuation. Altogether, 7,736 children were killed and 7,623 wounded in air-raids.

During the war there was a remarkable increase in public care for children, infants and their mothers. Schoolchildren got a daily milk ration and expectant mothers and babies got special allowances of cheap milk, cod liver oil, special foods and vitamin tablets, and advice from care clinics and welfare centres.

Society was now fully aware that children were the 'raw material of the Race'. There had been a recent expansion in the psychological study of children and attempts made to investigate the mind of the child and see things from his point of view. It was also recognised that childhood experiences had a crucial effect on the formation of personality, hence the youngster's home background was of fundamental importance.

Postwar society was determined to provide healthy, happy surroundings for the young, who became the focus of attention as never before. The remarkable change in attitudes since the beginning of the century was too much for one grandfather: 'I was born into an unfortunate generation. When I was a child I had to knuckle under to the grown-ups, and now I am a grown-up I have to knuckle under to the children.'

Further Reading
P. W. R. Foot, *The Child in the Twentieth Century*
G. Douglas, *London Street Games*
S. E. Ellacott, *A History of Everyday Things in England*, Vol. 5
Iona Opie, *The Lore and Language of Schoolchildren*

8   The Teen Age

Today's youngster enjoys a status unique in the history of English society. The tremendous importance which we attach to childhood is reflected in the complex network of child welfare provisions which have been created since the Second World War.

The postwar Labour government concentrated on improving youngsters' bodily health. In 1945 family allowances were given for the first time. A year later, as part of the new National Health Service local authorities had to help expectant and nursing mothers and their children under five. Health visitors were to give advice in maternity or child welfare centres or in the home on all aspects of pregnancy and infant training.

Today more than three out of five mothers attend centres for antenatal advice and three out of four babies are taken to welfare clinics. Here their physical progress is checked and any mental or physical handicaps can be detected. Mothers and babies can still get milk, orange juice, cod liver oil and vitamin tablets free or at reduced cost. Education authorities must provide schoolchildren with free medical and dental inspection, see that medical attention is given where necessary and that school nurses or health visitors follow up any suspected cases of neglect. Also available are clothing grants for the needy and transport for the disabled.

This policy has paid rich dividends. In 1870 the infant mortality rate was 150 for every 1,000 live births: in 1963 it was 21·7. Children are taller, heavier and healthier than ever. The medical officer reported in 1963 that well under one per cent of schoolchildren were in an unsatisfactory physical condition. Medical advances have saved many lives. For example, the use of vaccination and immunization, penicillin and other antibiotic drugs have prevented diseases previously deadly to children.

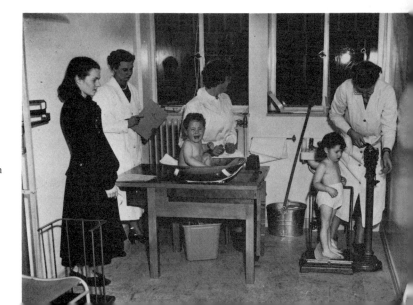

53 Youngsters at a child welfare clinic in 1952.

54 Lunchtime on a fine summer's morning at a day nursery.

Family planning   Many other factors have helped to produce today's strong, healthy youngsters. Mothers can devote more attention to their children since families are smaller in number, with a national average of 2·2 children per family. Contraception allows parents to plan the size of their family. The Victorian wealthy classes had used birth control but it was not till the 1920s when Dr Marie Stopes opened birth control clinics that the problems were freely discussed. The slogan of the birth control societies was 'Children by choice not chance' and the National Birth Control Council continued to open more clinics. The Council changed its name in 1939 to the Family Planning Association, which now has about 1,000 clinics. The Family Planning Act of 1967 has granted permission to local authorities to provide free birth control advice if they so wish.

In smaller families more money can be spent on the child and the rise in the standard of living and wages has made this even easier. Shorter working hours enable the father to spend more time with the child. Handbooks on child-care are best-sellers, the most popular being Dr Benjamin Spock's *Baby and Child Care*— a book with an amazing world sale figure of 20 million copies since publication in 1946. Due to research work in psychology and sociology, parents are now aware that the child's mental health depends on affectionate parents and a stable home background.

The postwar government investigated and then introduced laws to protect children from harmful surroundings. Two committees investigated 'the existing methods of providing for children . . . deprived of a normal home-life' who were in public care. They found there were 125,000 such children. Many were still in workhouses; some looked after only by old people or even cleaners. Most of the rest were in homes provided and managed by Public Assistance Committees. The majority were overcrowded, often containing double the intended numbers.

Deprived children

As a result of these findings the government decided on a completely new scheme for the deprived child, a simple, modern and humane one. It was outlined in the Children's Act of 1948. The scheme was to be operated by a single central department—the Home Office, with a new and enlarged children's branch. Each local authority had to appoint a Children's Committee and a Children's Officer. It was now the duty of every authority to receive into care anyone under 17 with-

55 Many special schools for children with physical disabilities have been built since the Second World War. Here a deaf youngster receives the benefits of advanced teaching techniques.

out a parent or guardian, who was abandoned or lost, or whose parents could not provide for him. The fact that authorities were not overwhelmed with the children of lazy or carefree parents says much for the country's new feeling of responsibility towards youngsters. Not only did the act mean a new deal for the youngster deprived of a decent home life, but for the first time real help was extended to the handicapped, disabled and mentally disturbed child.

In 1963 there were 65,000 children in the care of local authorities, with half of them living with foster parents. The rest lived in local authority homes or voluntary organised homes like Dr Barnardo's or the National Children's Home. The authorities have always tried hard to find a foster home. A Departmental Committee on Children and Young Persons report in 1960 laid great stress on the importance of family life to the growing child. Child social workers are now trained to recognise the symptoms of a maladjusted or inadequate family, and to know how it can be prevented from breaking up.

Juvenile delinquency

Wide powers have been given to juvenile courts to intervene when a child is reported to be in need of protection, including delinquent children or those in need of control. As a result of psychological research, the trend in juvenile courts has been towards guiding the delinquent child to adjust to society or else giving psychiatric treatment. The legal procedure for young offenders was revised in 1948. When an offence has been committed the child may be put on probation: he must see his probation officer regularly and keep out of further trouble. Failure to comply might mean a fine or an attendance centre order.

Attendance centres were started in 1948 as a way of controlling the activities of young offenders by making them report for a few hours of their spare time each week. Remand homes are for the custody of children before a court appearance or while waiting for a vacancy at an approved school. The broad aim of the latter schools is to teach difficult children to readjust for a return to the community. Detention centres are used to give a short, sharp warning to offenders who do not need Borstal training. Though Borstals are a punishment, their essential aim is to reform and educate the offender. Recently, magistrates have been more reluctant to commit offenders to Detention Centres or Borstal.

Throughout this scheme for dealing with offenders one can perceive the underlying motives of giving the child every chance; of refusing to label him as a criminal; and trying to reform him and enable him to adjust to the accepted standards of our society. All this is a far cry from the early nineteenth century solutions of hanging, imprisonment and transportation.

Education today

Our schools today are also a far cry from the harsh Victorian schools. During the Second World War the government determined to provide a new educational system as part of a general policy to improve children's opportunities in life. In 1944 Butler's Education Act replaced elementary education by primary education up to 11, after which most children were chosen for a grammar, technical or

56 Newcomers to a Borstal are exercised in forbidding surroundings in the 1950s. Borstals are intended to reform and educate the offender rather than treat him as a common criminal.

secondary modern school on the basis of an examination nicknamed the 'eleven-plus'. In the 1950s pupils in some areas were not selected—there was no examination and all attended comprehensive schools. For some time the Labour party has been urging authorities to change to this system of comprehensive education, in the hope that every child will thereby get equal educational opportunities.

We have space to mention only a few of the changes which have transformed schools and made them into much happier places. Jean Piaget, a child psychologist, has investigated the nature of children's thinking and his findings have stimulated new approaches to the teaching of primary school children. Many primary schools use new methods for the teaching of reading, and children learn by making their own discoveries in mathematics, science and field studies, instead of merely remembering what teacher says. In the secondary schools relationships between pupils and teachers are generally more relaxed and natural, the range of subjects taught has widened, a large proportion of pupils stay on to take the new Certificate of Secondary Education examination, and all receive advice from the Youth Employment Officer before leaving school.

Teenagers
Since the 1950s adults have used the new word 'teenager' to describe older children. Earlier in the century all young people were called children (or sometimes 'cock sparrows' or 'young shavers') and they were treated as such until they left school at an early age, usually 14, when immediately they were expected to act as adults. Adult attitudes have changed since then for many reasons. As we have seen, young people stay at school till they are much older: one can hardly call a 15-year-old a child any more. Also, young people are bigger and more physically mature than ever, they are better educated and encouraged to develop their own opinions since society no longer believes that tradition and old age are the main sources of wisdom.

Perhaps the decisive factor which has led society to distinguish older from younger children has been the new wealth and economic power which teenagers have enjoyed since the 1950s. In 1938 the average youth earned 26s a week, the average girl 18s 6d. By the 1950s the earnings of teenagers had increased in value by 50 per cent and their spending capacity by 100 per cent, and that is after allowing for the drop in the value of money. Adult wages rose only half as fast. In the year 1964–65 teenagers between 15 and 21 spent £900 million, and they contributed a quarter of the total amount spent by the country on consumer goods. Many young people still at school did part-time jobs, such as shop assistants, delivering newspapers or groceries and many teenagers received good pocket money from their parents.

This new wealth has had two important effects. The image of the teenager as a special group was fostered by advertising, as consumer industries sought to sell a vast new range of goods specially for young people. Secondly, teenagers' wealth has given them the chance to follow their own fashions in clothes, music and

57 A dance hall in the 'fifties and a teddy-boy 'moon-dancing' with his girlfriend. The 'teddy-boy style' symbolized the early stages of teenage rebellion against adult society and standards.

entertainment and thus emphasise the distinction between themselves and other age-groups.

The first signs of adolescent fashions appeared in the late 1940s with the popularity of the wide-shouldered jackets of the 'spiv' suit, and the craze among a large minority for jiving and jazz-clubs. True distinctiveness came in the mid fifties with the 'Teddy Boys' and their long, brylcreem-shiny hair, drainpipe trousers, long jackets with velvet cuffs and collars, boot-lace ties and thick crepe-soled shoes. Though a minority, they did represent, in its most extreme form, the general mood of teenage rebellion against the attitudes of adult society. More commonly, this rebellion made itself felt in many homes with arguments about

Fashions and fads

83

dress, boy-friends and late nights, as parents naturally showed reluctance to relinquish the complete authority over their children they had so far enjoyed. Today, parents are generally prepared to give a measure of freedom without a fight and accept the teenager's right to choose at least his own clothes, music and entertainment.

Some adolescent amusements barely changed after the war. Comics remained extremely popular with youngsters of all ages. The American 'horror' comic, imported during the war years, continued to be widely read, as did the boys' adventure comics, like *Adventure* and *Champion* and the comic-strips *Beano* and *Dandy*. In 1950 an estimated £5 million a year was being spent on comics. In this year, a new 'high quality' comic called *Eagle* was launched, followed by *Girl*,

58 Three examples of teenage cults. On the left a boy and a girl 'mod', almost identical in their appearance. In the centre a 'hippie', and on the right the more recent phenomenon, the 'skin-head', with his boots and braces and dislike of the hippies.

59 Girls' fashions – a mini skirt worn under a maxi coat. The increasing spending power of children today has benefited the fashion trade in particular.

Robin and *Swift*; but their high popularity was short-lived and in the sixties girls began to prefer romantic stories in *Marty, Mirabelle* and *Roxy* and recently the teenage magazines like *Honey* modelled on women's journals. Boys turned to football papers like *Buchan's Football Monthly* or the more recent *Shoot* and *Striker*, and to adult practical magazines and papers on hobbies. Among younger children information periodicals like *Knowledge* and *Look and Learn* have sold well.

Youngsters of all ages have shown a growing interest in non-fictional books. This trend is mainly explained by the presence of television. Imagination is satisfied by hours of fantasy and adventure stories each week. The few documentary and factual programmes tend to encourage children to read more on the subjects.

Nowadays libraries try hard to attract young readers with separate children's libraries and bright, modern decor. Many local authorities too have begun to provide other recreational facilities for young children who can no longer play safely on the busy streets or whose parents are at work. There are playgroups, parks, adventure playgrounds, junior clubs, and play-centres.

For teenagers there are still the Scouts and Guides, with half a million members each in 1963, or the Boys' Brigade and Junior Red Cross, though these organizations are undeniably losing a number of members now to voluntary service movements to help the aged, sick and homeless, like Task Force and Shelter.

The favourite interests of teenagers since the fifties have been youth and beat clubs, fashion, dancing and music. There was the rock 'n roll music, the 'top twenty' and the coffee bars of the late fifties. The sixties were heralded by beat music, Italian style suits, 'winkle-picker' shoes, girls' stiletto heels, and then in 1962 came the Beatles and the Rolling Stones, with screaming fans and Beatlemania reaching their peak in 1964.

Rival groups of teenagers emerged, each with distinctive clothes. 'Mods' dressed in smart suits or wore casual clothes, rode scooters and hated rock music, whereas 'Rockers' wore leather, preferred motor-bikes and enjoyed occasional Bank holiday 'punch-ups' with Mods. Since then, there have been rapidly-changing fashions in clothes, including the girls' trouser suit, mini-skirt, maxi-coat and knee-length boots. Jeans have been consistently popular with all youngsters since the fifties.

Today clothes are not used so much as a uniform, though there still are distinctive groups. 1968 was the summer of the 'flower' children with bells, beads and psychedelic music. A year later 'skinheads' marched in with boots and braces and a hatred of 'greasers' and 'hippies'.

Unsolved problems

The violence and vandalism of some juvenile groups is a sharp reminder that, though society can congratulate itself on the enormous improvement in the quality of child life, many serious problems remain to be tackled. A third of all indictable offences are committed by people under 17, and a half by people under 21. Juvenile delinquency is not decreasing.

More research and greater government provision in the field of mental health are essentials for future improvements in child health. There is far too little provision for child guidance clinics to deal with the emotionally maladjusted. Too many youngsters still suffer from a harmful or inadequate home environment. Drug-taking and vandalism are clear signs that many young people have not been able to adjust satisfactorily to our society. R. Weiner's recent survey of 1,000 London school-leavers classified 5·4 per cent as drug-takers. A survey of Midlands students in higher education put the percentage of those who had used drugs at 9·5 per cent. Those on 'hard drugs' are in desperate need of treatment, yet the provision for such centres has been slow.

There are still many court cases of mistreatment by parents, for instance, a Bradford couple in 1970 found guilty of the 'horrifying neglect' of the 15-month-old girl whose weight had increased by only 12 ounces since birth and who looked like a Belsen victim. According to the Child Poverty Action Group there are still about three-quarters of a million British children living around or below the poverty line. This organisation found that in 1969 only four per cent of working fathers, who were entitled to free welfare foods for their youngsters actually claimed them.

The provision of day-nurseries is grossly inadequate. Furthermore, in 1970, 70,188 children were in the care of local authorities, of whom 30 per cent had to live in authority homes, hostels and nurseries.

However, the world problems are much more staggering. Three-quarters of the child population live in poor countries, most have an inadequate education and pictures of Biafran or Indian children pot-bellied from hunger are a sadly familiar sight. Perhaps they remind us of the fate of many Victorian youngsters, who were exploited mercilessly as cheap labour; of Tudor children almost certain to die of disease and starvation in infancy; and of medieval infants killed by parents unable to support them.

Since British society has at last been successful in wiping out most of these evils, we now ought to support more generously the United Nations' Children's Fund in its fight to give the world's youngsters a happy childhood.

Further Reading
Allan Sillitoe, *The Loneliness of the Long-Distance Runner*
Colin MacInnes, *Absolute Beginners*
Central Office of Information, *Children in Britain*
Peter Laurie, *The Teenage Revolution*
John Mays, *The Young Pretenders*

General histories, useful for most chapters
Elizabeth Godfrey, *English Children in the Olden Time*
Sylvia Lynd, *English Children*
Magdalen King-Hall, *The Story of the Nursery*

Desirée Edwards-Rees, *Family Life in Britain*
L. Stoddard, *The Story of Youth*
Ivy Pinchbeck and Margaret Hewitt, *Children in English Society* Vol. 1
Robert Wood, *Children 1773–1890*
Leslie Daiken, *Children's Games*
Frederick J. Darton, *Children's books in England: 5 centuries of Social Life*
Iris Brooke, *English children's costume since 1775*

Date-Line of Child Life

1500–1600 Average life expectation 30 years
1536 Every parish can take begging children aged 5–14 and apprentice them in unskilled jobs
1552 Christ's Hospital opens—accommodation for 500 destitute children
1563 Statute of Artificers—7 years' apprenticeship to be the national and compulsory system of training for all industrial classes
1572 Imprisonment for adolescents over 14 years of age found begging
1576 Local authorities can punish the parents of an illegitimate child. No mention of the child
1579 Scots Poor Law—anyone can seize the children of vagrants and make them work without wages
1500–1600 Four weeks' annual holiday for grammar school pupils. Some children of the wealthy attending university at 12
1597 Act to make the parish responsible for all destitute and orphan children: basis of the Poor Law till 1834

1610 One year in a House of Correction for the mother of an illegitimate child
1680 Sheffield Scissorsmiths—a report of apprentices becoming lame through overwork results in their working day being limited to 14 hours
c. 1696 *Cinderella*, *Red Riding Hood*, *Sleeping Beauty*, *Puss in Boots* and other traditional tales written down and published for the first time
1698 Society for Promoting Christian Knowledge (SPCK) is founded
1,600 charity schools opened in the next 30 years

1702 Royal Asylum of St Ann's Society for Destitute Children—the oldest surviving orphanage in Britain
1700–1750 Three-quarters of the nation's children die before the age of six
1741 Foundling Hospital for abandoned children
1744 John Newberry publishes the first book solely for children *A Little Pretty Pocket Book*
1758 Female Orphan Asylum for destitute young girls 9–12 years old
c. 1760 The first jigsaw-puzzles
c. 1775 The 'Empire' frock—the first dress designed specially for children
1778 No paupers to remain as apprentices after 21 years of age
1780 Robert Raikes starts the first Sunday school
1793 Pupils revolt and occupy Winchester school

1802 The Health and Morals of Apprentices Act

1803 Official figure of 195,000 permanent child paupers

1813 James Catnach begins printing chapbooks specially for youngsters

1817 500 chimney-sweep boys in London alone

1818 Joseph Pounds starts teaching 'ragged' children in his shoemaker's shop

1824 Patent for a doll which says 'Mamma' and 'Papa'. The young Victoria (later Queen) has 132 dolls

1832 Sadler's Committee: further enquiry into the working conditions of factory children

1833 Factory Act: children under nine must not work; those under 13 limited to 9 hours a day. Inspectors appointed

1832–1842 Only half the children of working mothers in the cotton industry live to five years of age

1838 Provision of a separate wing for the detention of children at Parkhurst Prison

Oliver Twist focuses attention on the plight of workhouse children

1842 First report by the Commissioners on the Employment of Children. Result—the Mines and Collieries Act

1844 The Ragged School Union formed

1846 First English translation of Hans Christian Andersen's fairy tales

1847 Act to limit the work of women and young persons in the textile factories to 10 hours daily

The first use of anaesthetics for child birth

c. 1850 The crinoline being worn by upper-class children

1851 The Monthly Packet, the first magazine for nursery children

Magistrates can still sentence children to a punishment of 36 lashes

1854 The Reformatory Schools Act

1863 The Children's Employment Commission begins to issue reports on children in trades and manufactures

1867 Factory Acts Extension Act and the Workshops Regulation Act: cover children in all other trades

1870 Forster's Education Act: schools to be built wherever provision is inadequate

1872 Infant Life Protection Act: to licence and supervise baby-farmers

1876 Compulsory education for all under 10

1878 Consolidation Act: no child under eight to work in any trade; children between 8 and 13 can only work half time; young persons only 12 hours daily

1883 Boys' Brigade founded by Sir William Smith

Publication of R. L. Stevenson's Treasure Island

1884 Formation of the National Society for Prevention of Cruelty to Children (NSPCC). In 10 years it had dealt with 71,000 cases

1889 Children's Charter Act

1890   *Chips* and *Comic Cuts*, the first popular comics

1900   12 million children under 15 in a total British population of 38 million
        Children of 13 still free to drink beer in public houses
1900–1910   The national infant mortality rate falls by one third
1902   The first institution for Borstal training
1906   The provision of school meals for the needy
1907   The start of medical inspections of all schoolchildren
        The first Boy Scout camp
1908   Publication of Arthur Mee's *Children's Encyclopedia*
        Children's Act—consolidates recent acts for the rescue and training of slum
            children
        Death penalty abolished for children under 16
1909   Reports of children in the lace-making trade becoming blind because of
            work
1911   Introduction of first scheme for maternity benefits
1918   Local authorities given permission to help safeguard the health of mothers
            and babies
        Fisher's Education Act: school leaving age raised to 14
1919   Save the Children Fund begins
1922   Publication of *Just William* by Richmal Crompton
        No child under 12 to work at all
1926   Adoption Act: first legal safeguard for the adoption of children
1930   Youth Hostels Association (YHA) founded
1934   Cheap school milk
1935   The Rank Organisation makes the first education films for children
1937   *Dandy* first published; *Beano* a year later
1939   War children evacuated from 40 densely populated areas
1943   The first entertainment films made specially for young people
1944   Butler's Education Act: school leaving age raised to 15; three types of
            secondary schools with selection at 11
        United Nations Organisation formed: with a special agency to help
            children—The United Nations Children's Fund (UNICEF)
1945   Family Allowances Act
1946   National Health Service Act. Local authorities must provide help for
            expectant and nursing mothers and all children under five
1948   Children Act remodels the system of caring for children 'deprived of a
            normal home-life'
1950   Estimated £5 million per year being spent on comics
1959   United Nations adopts a 10-point 'Declaration of the Rights of the Child'
1960   Three-fifths of all criminal offenders are under 21 years of age
1963   Newsom Report on the average secondary school child—*Half Our Future*
1964   The infant death-rate below 20 per thousand for the first time ever

Young people spend £900 million on themselves
1966   The mini-skirt becomes popular
1967   Family Planning Act—local authorities can provide a birth control service
       for all
1969   Vote is given to young persons of 18
       Thousands of children die of starvation in the Biafran war

Index

The numerals in **bold** indicate the figure-numbers of the illustrations.

'Accomplishments', 33
Acts of Parliament:
    Children's, 1948, 79
    Children's Charter 1889, 47
    Education Acts: 1870 and 1876, 45
    1918, 70
    1944, 80
    Factory Acts: 1819 and 1833, 52
    1847, 55
    1867, 58
    1878, 56
    1891, 44
    Family Planning, 1967, 78
    Hanway's, 1767, 38
    Health and Morals of Apprentices, 1802, 52
    Maternity and Child Welfare, 1918, 67
    Mines and Collieries Regulation, 1842, 52
    Pauper children, 1536, 1547, 1816, 26–27, 39
    Reformatory Schools, 1854, 45
    Relief of the Poor, 1597, 19, 27
Apprentices, 15, 26–7, 39, 49–50
Arguments against child labour, 56
Arnold, Dr, 63
Attendance centres, 80

Baden-Powell, Robert, 73
Barnardo, Dr, 43, 80
Behaviour, 13, 24; **19**
Birth control, 78
Birth customs, 18
Birth rate, 64, 78
'Boarding-out', 13–14, 22
Books, children's, 31, 66, 73
Borstal system, 69, 80; **56**
Boys' Brigade, 47, 73, 87
'Breeching', 21
Brick workers, 55; **37**
Bridewell, 18–19
Bustle, 63

'Chambrières', 13–14
Charity schools, 40
Child Poverty Action Group, 88
Christ's Hospital, 18
Clothes, 29–30, 62–63, 73, 83, 87; **4, 43, 50, 59**
Coal-mine workers, 52, 55; **35, 36**
Comics, 66, 73, 85
Commissions of enquiry, 52, 55, 56, 67
Coram, Thomas, 37–38; **24**
Cottage workers, 49
Country children, 48–49; **32**
Crèches, 44; **28**
Crinoline, 63

Crossing sweepers, 47; **39**
Cruelty to children, 67–9, 88

Dame schools, 40; **25**
'Damoiselles' 14, **5**
Dancing, 73
Death-rates, 11, 18, 37–8, 67, 77
Defoe, Daniel, 48
Delinquency, juvenile, 39, 44–5, 69, 80, 87; **29**
Deportment, 33
Deprived children, 79
Diseases and illness, 18, 29, 52, 49, 61–2, 71, 77, 88
Doll's houses, 31; **21, 45**
Dressmaking, 55–6
Drug-taking, 88
'Dumping', 27

Education,
    medieval, 16–17
    Tudor and Stuart, 22; **11**
    eighteenth century, 34, 36, 40–41; **22**
    nineteenth century, 45–6, 58; **30**, 63–4
    twentieth century, 70, 73–4, 80–82
    girls' education, 13–14, 22–3, 33–4, 63
Evacuation, 74–5; **52**

Factory children, 49–52; **34**
Family life,
    medieval, 11–12; **1**
    Tudor and Stuart, 23–4; **13**
    nineteenth century, 64; **44**
    twentieth century, 78–9
Family Planning Association, 78
Fashion, teenage, 83, 87; **58**
Female Orphan Asylum, 39
Fielden, John, 52, 55
Fielding, Sir John, 39–40
Food, nursery, 61
Fordyce, Sir William, 29
Foundlings, 18–19, 37–38
Foundlings Hospital, 37–38
Free dinner societies, 47; **31**
Froebel, Friedrich, 60

Games, 16, 25, 30–1, 66; **7, 8, 15**
Gladstone, W. E., 47
Guides, Girl, 73, 87

'Half-time' system, 69–70
Hanway, Jonas, 38
Health, 74–5, 77, 88
Hobbies, 64–6

Horn book, 20; **10**
'Hurrier', 52, 54; **35**

Infants, treatment and feeding of, 9–11, 18, 28–9,
    43–4, 67; **2**

Libraries, children's, 73, 87
Locke, John, 48

Magazines, 66, 73, 87
Magdalen Hospital, 39
Marriage, 14
Maternity benefits, 44, 75
Medical inspection, 67, 74
Milk, school, 75

Names, 18
National Health Service, 77
National Society for the Prevention of Cruelty to
    Children, 47, 67–8
Needlework, 20, 22
Neglect, 11
Nurseries, 59–62, 77; **42**, **54**
Nurses, 20, 59; **2**, **40**, **47**

Offenders, young, 39, 44–5, **29**, 69, 80
Oliver Twist, 39
Orphanages and orphans, 19, 43, 80; **27**
Overseers, 51

Pages, boy, 13–14
'Pap', 28
Parents,
    medieval, 11–13
    Tudor and Stuart, 23–5
    Georgian, 30, **18**
    nineteenth century, 59–60, 63
    twentieth century, 78–79
Pauper children, 26–27, 42, 49–50; **3**
Peasant children, 15–16
Pestalozzi, Johann, 60
Piaget, Jean, 82
Portraits, child, 24–5
Pottery workers, 55
Pounds, John, 41; **26**
Prams, **41**
Psychology, child, 75–6, 78–9

Puritans, 24–5

Ragged schools, 41–42; **26**
Raikes, Robert, 40–1
Reading, 20, 30–1
Refuges, 42–3
Remedies for illness, 10, 61–2
Rhymes, nursery, 10–11, 20
Rocking horse, **42**
Rousseau, Jean-Jacques, 60

Samplers, 22; **12**
Save the Children Fund, 74
Schools, see Education.
School Attendance Officer, 70
Scouts, Boy, 73, 87; **51**
Shaftesbury, Earl of, 52, 55
Sloane, Dr. Hans, 29
Slum children, 67; **47**
Society for Promoting Christian Knowledge, 40
Society for the Protection of Infant Life, 44
Special schools, **55**
Statute of Artificers, 1563, 26
Stopes, Dr. Marie, 78
Street games, 70; **49**
Sunday schools, 40–1
Superstitions, 8–9
Swaddling, 10; **2**
Sweeps, child, 49, 58; **33**

Tailors, **38**
Teddy-boys, 83; **57**
Teenagers, 82–8
Tightlacing, 63
Toys, 16, 31–2, 64, 70; **20**, **21**, **46**
'Trapper', 52; **36**

Vagrant children, 39, 58
Voluntary societies, 47

War children, 74–5
Workers, child, 13–16, 48–58, 69–70; **6**
Workhouses, 38–9, 49–50, 67, 79
Workshop trades, 49, 55–6
World child problems, 88

Youth organisations, 73, 74, 87.